CHURCHILL:

Images of Greatness

Ronald A Smith

Published by Kevin Francis Publishing Ltd
85 Landcroft Rd
London SE22 9JS

Acknowledgements

A survey of this nature requires the tapping of a considerable number of sources and the assistance of many people and I would like to express my gratitude to all the following artists, colleges, museums, art galleries, magazines and all others who have generously provided photographs or information or allowed me to take photographs of material on the premises.

Vincent Apap
Elizabeth Baverstock
E. T. Bailey
Franta Belsky
Bernard Hailstone R.P.
Ivor Roberts-Jones C.B.E., R.A.
Astrid Zydower M.B.E.
John Leigh-Pemberton
Michael Sutty
Jean Broome
James Stuart (Bass)
James Blewitt
Brenda Lakey
Ted Slattery
Pat Bates
Don Cooke
Ralph Prout
Donald Forbes C.B.E.
William Harvey
Derek Ransley
Yashsa Bereseina (Intercol)
Ian & Rita Smythe (Britannia Antiques)
J. Eric Engstrom
Richard Copeland (Copeland Spode)
Major Taylor-Smith
Fred Hambrook Colton

Ardath
Philip Morris
Carreras Rothman
Dept. of Information, Malta
National Museum Van de Speelkart, Turnhout
Halcyon Days
E. W. & P. M. Page
Imperial War Museum
Brunei Museum
Bromley Library
Government Art Collection
National Gallery
National Portrait Gallery (Archives)
Scottish Portrait Gallery
Beaverbrook Art Gallery, N.B.
Smithsonian Institute, Washington
British Maritime Museum
Durban History Museum
Public Archives, Nova Scotia

National Liberal Club
Guildhall Library
Trinity House Lighthouse Service
Worshipful Company of Grocers
Worshipful Company of Makers of Playing Cards
The National Trust
Hastings Town Council
Deal Town Council
Dover Town Council
Phototheque Municipale, Luxembourg
Fridhelskampens Veteraner, Denmark
Madame Tussauds London
Madame Tussauds Amsterdam
Louis Tussaud Copenhagen
Deptment of the Environment
The Churchill hotel, London
Crown Agents for the Colonies
H.M. Post Office
Societe Jersiaise
The History in Porcelain Company
Spinks
After the Battle Magazine
James Gardner (3D Concepts)
Frost & Reed
Mappin & Webb
Garrard
Frank Sinclair Ltd
Courtaulds Institute of Art, University of London
Kent University
Bristol University
Churchill College, Cambridge University
Royal Doulton
B.E.L. (Birmingham) Ltd
Illustrated London News
Burgess & Leigh Ltd
A. & C.Black Ltd
Cassell & Co.
Whitbread Breweries
Brooke Bond
Imperial Tobacco

Production and Editorial, Francis Salmon
Design and Compilation, ScanGraphics
Word Processing by Jan Chignal
Cover by Francis Salmon and Trevor Leek
Oil Painting by John Standeven

To Audrey

Contents

About the Author

Ronald Albert Smith was at the impressionable age of ten when the second world war began. He and his fellow schoolboys became great admirers of Churchill. This admiration sprang from those early war years when after every major speech by the Prime Minister their enthusiastic English Master gave it next day as a dictation exercise. Far from being a chore, the boys found tremendous inspiration from Churchill's words and avidly took up their pens!

The author is convinced that without Churchill as war time leader, Britain would have lost the war.

Ronald lives in North London with his wife, Audrey and younger daughter, Claire. He is avidly interested in Churchilliana and other political and royal memorabilia. After 27 years working for the Midland Bank he has now turned his antique and collectables interest into a full time occupation.

Preface

The life of Sir Winston Churchill has of necessity been the subject of an enormous quantity of literature in many books printed and re-printed over the years, and there will no doubt be many more books to be placed one day upon the shelves next to the distinguished volumes concerning him. There may be a great deal of repetition among these volumes, but each attempts to bring us a new aspect of Churchill; another side to the many facets of his nature and being. There is no question mark over what he did, more a fascination over who he was, where he came from and what gave rise to such heady heights of greatness. The historian, the student and the general reader will learn of Churchill's greatness in any of the prolific volumes which present themselves to the enquiring public, but there is one area which has been surprisingly neglected over the years, and it is this area which is to be examined in the pages of this book.

Here you will find a different Churchill — a Churchill seen through the inspired eyes of artists, be he painted, modelled, cast or sculptured. It is the combined work of these artists which builds for us an as yet uncharted aspect of Churchill, the Churchill we most know in public life.

The diverse portrayal of Churchill through the minds of these artists is equalled only by the many roles which Churchill undertook throughout his life. From the early artistic representations of the 1900's through to those of the present day, we see not only the Winston Churchill in his 'finest hour', but also the Winston Churchill of the Boer War, the Winston Churchill of the Great War, the Winston Churchill who was Chancellor of the Exchequer during the twenties and the Churchill who warned of immense dangers throughout the 1930s.

Commemoration of Churchill's greatest feats is to be found in the abundance of artistic impressions which make up the world of Churchilliana, ranging from the humble cigarette card issued in the Boer War to the superb vases, busts and medallions made to commemorate the centenary of his birth.

Churchill will surely be regarded as 'the man of the century', and this book provides a unique reference to the many means and methods by which the peoples of the world have recognised this. Apart from the wealth of material from Great Britain there are many fine images from other countries. Churchill was an enormous inspiration to the British people during the war, a demigod who spoke articulately for his 'Island Race' and inspired them to face with confidence the greatest challenge in their long and glorious history. Likewise the conquered peoples of Europe looked to him as the man who would free them from their oppressive captors. He did not fail. The sheer quantity and variety of souvenirs, commemoratives, utilty items, statues and sculptures provide a measure of the regard and affection in which he was held.

Many of the pieces illustrated formed part of an exhibition held recently at the Cabinet War Rooms, Storey Gate, London. These rooms, steeped in the war time atmosphere of the forties, proved to be a most fitting site for the display. Whether the memento was cheap or expensive, rare or one of many, the reason for its production was the same — a tribute to serve as a perpetual reminder of the fabulous man who was Churchill.

CHAPTER ONE
The Young Statesman

'On 30th November 1874 at Blenheim Place, The Lady Randolph Churchill prematurely, a son.' This brief message in 'The Times' announced to the British Public that Winston Leonard Spencer Churchill had arrived. Hasty and impetuous in his own life time, it seems that even in birth he had no time to wait.

His mother was the beautiful Jenny, 20 year old daughter of a successful American businessman, Leonard Jerome. His father was Lord Randolph Churchill, the aloof and brilliant, third son of the seventh Duke of Marlborough. This aristocratic pedigree combined with American drive and determination to ensure generous favour to the new born child.

Throughout his life Churchill loved his mother dearly, and though they were often apart, he declared that she "shone for me like the evening star...".

Until he was seven he was looked after by his nanny, Mrs Everest, to whom he was devoted and in whose care he was very happy. All this changed when he was sent to boarding school near Ascot. There he endured two bitter years at the hands of a brutal headmaster. Winston's work suffered and his health deteriorated before he was taken from the school and put into the charge of two elderly ladies in Brighton.

It was intended to send him from there to Eton College, but his mother thought that Harrow, 'the school on the Hill', would be better for his health. He gained access to the school, not through academic brilliance, but largely because of the fame of his father.

In fact Winston made a poor showing at the entrance examination and was unable to answer any questions in the Latin Paper. The story related by him is that he put his name at the top of the paper and then wrote the figure one in brackets. A few smudges and a blot completed his paper, which was mercifully taken away after two hours.

The long time that he spent in the lowest form proved to be of enormous benefit as he received a thorough grounding in the English language. He very much admired his English Master, who taught the subject as no other master had taught it. It was here that the foundation of Churchill's great mastery of the English language was laid, albeit a period in which he spent three years in the third form because he was not considered bright enough to move up.

Churchill had a prodigious memory and while in the lower form he gained a prize for the recitation of 1200 lines of Macauley's 'Lays of Ancient Rome' without a single mistake. Such remarkable memory enabled Churchill to memorise his own speeches in later years.

The First Duke of Marlborough, illustrious ancestor of Winston Churchill.

Blenheim Palace, birthplace of Winston.

Lord Randolph thought Winston a relatively backward child, despaired of him, and discouraged suggestions that he take up a career in law. Seeing that his young son had a passion for playing with toy soldiers he enquired if he would like to go into the army. Winston said he would, and the boy's future was settled.

It took Winston three attempts (with special tuition) to pass into Sandhurst. At the military establishment he had a fresh start and could substitute the tedium of Latin and French for organised games. Such 'games' were in the field of war — tactics, fortification, map-making and military law and the art of leadership and command. In the sporting field there was gymnastics and riding.

Through his father he met the leading politicians of the day and gained a deep knowledge of national and international affairs. He longed for a deeper relationship with his father, but this was not possible. If ever Winston showed the slightest sign of comradeship he was immediately rebuffed. Winston recalled only having had three or four conversations at length with his father, whom he admired greatly.

At Sandhurst Winston passed out eighth in a batch of of one hundred and fifty and was gazetted to the 4th Hussars. He was fond of listening to the stories by his senior officers of daring deeds, and he longed for the chance to taste military action and go to war.

His first 'taste of war' was in Cuba in the 1895 guerilla insurgence against the Spanish authorities. However, this was not in the capacity of soldier but as a war correspondent for the Daily Graphic. He was attached to a Spanish battalion and experienced his first taste of threat from gunfire and the "smell of death" on his twenty-first birthday.

This war lasted only three days, but Churchill, who was on leave from the army during this period, gained invaluable experience. He was awarded the Spanish Order of Military Merit 1st Class for his endeavours, his first decoration, and the emergence of Winston Churchill as a prominent personality had begun. One other less striking but no less important addition to the image of Churchill that we all know was the passion he developed for long, fat, Cuban cigars!

The following year, in 1896, Churchill's regiment was sent to India and at Bangalore he enjoyed the military and sporting life. He was not just a sportsman though, and aware of the limitations of his knowledge, he read widely the works of Aristotle, Plato, Gibbon, MacAulay and Darwin. After almost one year in India without much action he took the opportunity for leave of three months and a return to England.

During his leave he was thrilled to read of the revolt of the Pathan tribesmen on the Indian Frontier and with his appetite for action whetted, he determined to return to India. Reminding General Sir Bindon Blood of his promise to take him on any future expedition on the Indian Frontier, Churchill managed to get to the scene of war. But not in uniform. Though Bindon Blood was at the head of the newly formed Malakand Field Force of three Brigades fighting to supress an uprising of Pathan tribesmen, there were no army vacancies and Churchill had to be content with travelling with the army as war correspondent.

Having won leave of absence from his own regiment, Churchill became correspondent to the 'Pioneer', an Indian newspaper, and his mother arranged for the 'Daily Telegraph' to publish his letters at £5 per column.

The Pathans were a savage, ferocious tribe and Churchill was almost slain on one occasion by a tribesman wielding a sword. He carried eight wounded men to safety and braved himself on the front line at the height of the battle.

Churchill was very critical of his Senior Officers who were often angry at his reports but they could do nothing to stop him, and Churchill went on to write his first book, 'The Malakand Field Force', which was highly acclaimed and even read by Edward, Prince of Wales, who wrote congratulating Churchill on his success. Soon Winston was thirsting for adventure again.

Conveniently, for Churchill perhaps, fighting broke out in the Sudan. Sir Herbert Kitchener was the head of a British and Egyptian force of 20,000 men preparing to advance on Khartoum, from there to crush the Dervishes and avenge General Gordon's death. Kitchener, aware of Churchill's condemnation of senior officers in his reports, opposed his presence, but by headstrong efforts and 'pulling strings in the right places', Churchill was attached as an unpaid Lieutenant to the 21st Lancers on the understanding that death or injury to him would be no responsibility of the British Army. He was engaged by the 'Morning Post' to be their official correspondent, writing a series of articles for £15 per column.

At the battle of Omdurman, Kitchener's Army was heavily outnumbered by the Dervishes, though it possessed superior weapons. Within one hour of battle, 20,000 Dervishes lay dead or wounded. The Omdurman charge, in which Churchill led his troop, was the last of its kind, and the famous victory was appropriately related by Churchill to avid readers at home in Britain.

With the uprising quashed, Churchill returned to England and undertook his history of the Sudan campaign on the journey, a work entitled, 'The River War.' His book was a great success, revealing more of his literary talents and displaying his depth of talent as an analytical historian.

Churchill now hoped to win a seat in Parliament, but his first attempt for the Conservative Party failed when he was defeated at Oldham in 1899.

Before Churchill had another opportunity to stand for election to Parliament, another conflict overseas attracted his attention. For months the tension between Boer and Briton had been simmering. The arms build up of the Boers and the increasing numbers of British troops created the ground for hostility

Mr WINSTON CHURCHILL

The earliest souvenir of Churchill, war correspondent in South Africa.

and a full scale war. Churchill was inevitably South Africa bound; this time as full-blown correspondent to the 'Morning Post' — and at a record salary of £250 per month — the highest salary ever offered for such work.

Although Churchill was a civilian in South Africa, he travelled with a small army force on a journey by armoured train. After fourteen miles the train was suddenly derailed by a shell wedged on the track. Churchill supervised the freeing of the engine from the trucks which allowed the train to steam along at a slow pace with dead and wounded soldiers aboard. Able bodied troops walked alongside the engine while Churchill was in a cab crammed with men. As the train picked up speed, the walking troops were left behind. In the absence of a commanding officer, Churchill ordered the train to be stopped, some three hundred yards between the train itself and the soldiers intended to protect it. As Churchill made his way on foot from the train to the soldiers he was intercepted by three armed Boers, one of them mounted, who took him prisoner. After three days marching and travelling by train, Churchill and other British prisoners were locked up in state schools at Pretoria.

One month later Churchill made a spectacular escape, hiding until a guard's back was turned and then climbing over a wall. The Boers put out 'wanted' posters in both English and Afrikaans offering a reward of £25 for WinstonChurchill, dead or alive. They failed to find him. After a few days down a disused mine full of rats, Churchill concealed himself in a wagon loaded with wool which arrived in Portugese East Africa. Some days later he reached Durban and was given a tumultuous reception. Now a hero who had thwarted the intentions of the enemy he was soon given an unpaid commission in the British Army.

His stirring adventures, capture and escape and his colourful reporting of the Boer War won him many admirers in Britain. Growing fame led to his inclusion in 'Ogden's Golden Guinea Series' of cigarette cards, issued in 1900. This firm printed a picture of him in several different sizes, on the reverse being described as a war correspondent. At the same time another firm, Cohen, Weenen & Co, featured him in army uniform and bush hat in their own series of famous people.

Convinced that he was a man of destiny and that his future was to be in politics, Churchill used his newly-won fame as a springboard for his second attempt to gain a seat in Parliament, again as a Conservative. This was 1900, and such was his popularity that he had a choice of eleven seats for which to stand. He chose Oldham and won his seat by a very slim majority of 222 votes.

At the age of 26 and established already as a national figure, an early tribute was paid to Churchill by Foley China who included him in their series of teapots depicting in caricature prominent politicians. The series was issued about 1900 and was known as the Intarsio collection. Similarly teapotted contempories of Churchill were such famous men as Joseph Chamberlain,

Famous father of a famous son; Lord Randolph, who died aged 47.

The first ceramic souvenir, the very rare Foley Teapot made about 1900.

Balfour, Lord Roseberry, even Kruger. The teapots are uniform in shape and size and colour, with the head and shoulders of the statesman on the lid. All the teapots are very rare, the Churchill example exceptionally so.

He was in great demand as a speaker, addressing large audiences and receiving between £100 and £300 for each booking. Before taking his seat in Parliament he raised some much needed cash by giving a series of lectures throughout an American tour. In addition to the payment from this trip, which totalled £10,000, he gained very valuable experience as a speaker.

It was obvious that in Parliament he would be compared with his brilliant father who had been Chancellor of the Exchequer and many well known people were present to hear his maiden speech. It soon became evident that he was not afraid to speak his mind, and even attack his own Tory Ministers.

Fellow MPs felt that he was going too far, and, over time, he made many political enemies, a gulf widening between his personal views and the policies of the party. Over Joseph Chamberlain's attempts to bring in tariffs on goods from outside the Dominions and Colonies, Churchill rebelled and in May 1904 crossed the floor of the House and joined the Liberals.

In 1906 the Liberals won the General Election, and Churchill was now representing the Constituency of Manchester North West. In this Government he received his first appointment, which was as Under Secretary of State for the Colonies. He held this Office when his youthful portrait appeared in a very rare set of cigarette cards, 'Modern Statesmen', issued by Hignetts Butterfly cigarettes. His parliamentary progress was to be faithfully charted for the next few years by cigarette cards. Whilst today these cards would not be particularly significant, it must be remembered that in the days before television and radio, when literacy among the masses was low and the press did not generally cater for them, such cards gave invaluable information, simply and with pictures for reference.

Churchill scored another literary success when his biography of his father, 'Lord Randolph Churchill,' was published in 1906.

Two years later, at the age of thirty-four, he became President of the Board of Trade. He was now well established in the public eye, as soldier, writer and politician. In this new capacity, Churchill was responsible for the introduction of Labour Exchanges throughout Britain.

Many held him to be a confirmed bachelor also, but such speculation ended with his marriage to Clementine Hosier in 1908.

His career moved ahead swiftly and in 1910 he became Home Secretary. This is one of the highest of government posts, and from this time on Churchill was regarded as a future Prime Minister by many people.

In January 1911 a gang of criminals from Latvia, having shot and killed three policemen in London a few weeks previously, were traced to a house in Stepney, East London. The house was soon besieged by hundreds of soldiers and police, and Churchill, always interested in any exciting situation, visited the scene during the siege which ended in the house burning down and two of the gang burning to death. Some dramatic postcards of the scene were printed, one of which shows the Home Secretary huddled in a gateway at the head of a group of soldiers, peering round a corner at the edge of the house.

Churchill's spell as Home Secretary was brief, for in 1911, with the undercurrents of war being felt, the Prime Minister, Herbert Asquith, appointed him the First Lord of the Admiralty. His job was to put the Navy into a state of constant readiness in case of attack. As First Lord he was brilliantly successful, among his major reforms being the modernisation of the Navy from plans made by Admiral Lord Fisher, the First Sea Lord, by converting ships from coal to oil burning engines. He commissioned faster ships and bigger guns, and soon realised the tremendous potential of air power, in 1913 forming the Royal Naval Air Corps, which eventually became the Fleet Air Arm.

Churchill was certain that war would soon develop, and Germany and Britain vied with one another in building up massive naval forces. As First Lord of the Admiralty, Churchill earned depiction on several series of cigarette cards issued around 1914. These were 'War Portraits' by R. J. Lea Ltd., 'Britain's Defenders,' by Sissors and Wills, and 'Silk Portraits' by Godfrey Phillips.

The long expected war came after Germany invaded France and Belgium, refusing to withdraw her troops. Churchill had already mobilised his fleet before the declaration of war, and confidence in him as a leader was reinforced when, along with other military, naval and political leaders of the day he was depicted on patriotic postcards, often with a Union Jack and sometimes with a bulldog or a British Lion. Typical of these cards is the series, 'Men of the Moment', 1914, with a card showing Churchill's photograph against the British Flag.

Churchill had a very fertile and inventive mind and is credited with having been the inspiration behind the development of the tank. On seeing the trenches in the Great War he had naval engineers design an armoured car capable of crossing them. They produced a vehicle on a catapillar tread, which was successfully demonstrated and he ordered twelve for the Royal Navy.

One of the earliest, possibly the first wartime ceramic souvenir concerning Churchill, was an earthenware plate bearing the backstamp, 'Cetem Ware', the mark of C. T. Maling & Son. The plate has a cartoon of Churchill by Miguet and it was part of a series of plates depicting in caricature, notable personalities of the day. They were issued about 1914 and are extremely rare.

A splendid souvenir from the early war period was a large square cloth on which is presented a gallery of portraits of allied Sovereigns, distinguished soldiers, sailors and statesmen of those days. Again, in his capacity as First

Lord of the Admiralty, Churchill is among the eminent people depicted. The violated treaty of 1839, signed and sealed by six European powers, which guaranteed Belgium independence, was displayed in the centre of a group of allied flags. Since the treaty had been violated by the aggressive behaviour of Germany, it was referrred to as a 'Scrap of Paper', and the treaty itself was being used in the propaganda effort.

Not much else was made concerning Churchill during the First World War, no doubt because of his early resignation from the Government and his subsequent temporary fading from the limelight. An item that was produced before his fall, however, was a small, white bust showing him in military dress, complete with a row of medals. This scarce item is one of a series of war personalities; it is in very fine china and marked, 'Shelley, late Foley'. Inscribed on the front of the pedestal is 'Rt. Hon. Winston Churchill, First Lord of the Admiralty'. A similar bust was unmarked but bears the name of the sculptor, Lawton. A number of very interesting sets of wooden caricatures of allied statesmen and military and naval leaders came from the workshops of Lord Roberts in South London. These sets comprised some 20 figures and were hand-carved by disabled servicemen. A splendid carved and coloured figure of Churchill, seated and skirted as Britannia, is included in the series which is called, 'Men Who Matter'.

In 1915 the tragedy of Gallipoli (in which Britain and her allies suffered the terrible losses of 200,000 men killed and wounded) threw a shadow of doom across Churchill's future, causing his career to founder and halt, for he was one of the chief advocates of the disastrous campaign Under his leadership, an attempt had been made to force a passage through the fortified Dardenelles, and land troops on the Gallipoli Peninsular. If successful, many advantages would follow — German pressure on the Russian front would be reduced, Turkey would be effectively knocked out of the war and the stalemate on the Western front would turn in favour of the allies with the consequent transfer east of German troops — the war would be shortened by years. After initial success though, disagreement between the Admirals and Generals resulted in failure, culminating in the decision to evacuate the troops. The withdrawal was costly, not only in money terms, but in loss of life and thousands of casualties. Churchill bore the brunt of the blame for the tragedy and was compelled to resign his Office.

In order to maintain an active position in the war and still be able to influence its direction, Churchill accepted the relatively minor appointment of Chancellor of the Duchy of Lancaster. This office gave him a seat on the War Council and through it he remained a member of the War Cabinet. As Chancellor he was clearly frustrated and in growing despair. However, from the arduous and responsible toil at the Admiralty he now passed into the idleness of his sinecure office. To lessen the tedium and his resulting depressions he began to develop his talent for painting. Longing to play a more active part in the war, he took up a post in France as Major Churchill.

The German enemy was quick to seize on the apparent failure of the First Lord and in mockery of him they cast a portentous medal, designed and struck in iron by W. Eberbach. Some forty years before he was created Knight of the Garter, this medallion prophetically bears the inscription, "SIR WINSTON CHURCHILL DEM SEEGEWALTIGEN", (Sir Winston Churchill Ruler of the Seas). The obverse design is a nude warrior, believed to be Siegfried, fighting with a monster representing British Sea Power.

He is featured holding the rank of Major in a set of cigarette cards entitled, 'Notabilities', issued about 1916. Soon he was Colonel Churchill and commanded a battalion of the Royal Scots Fusiliers and although there was some initial scepticism of him he soon won the respect of his men. He struck a notable figure in his distinct light blue French steel helmet as he visited his mens' position in the trenches three time each day. After some months of trench warfare his battalion was amalgamated with another and he was without command. The lack of a command and growing pressure from his colleagues in Parliament finally persuaded him to return to Parliament as a back-bencher.

However, a Dardenelles Commission was appointed to inquire into the disaster which had so upset Churchill's political career, and he was relieved to find that the Commission attached no blame to his part in the fiasco.

In 1917 Churchill was appointed Minister of Munitions, succeeding Lloyd George who became Prime Minister. In this position he was responsible for the production of enormous quantities of armaments and munitions. The job took him to France many times, and on a number of occasions to America, where he developed strong diplomatic ties. In acknowledgement of his hard work in encouraging American involvement, he was awarded the American Distinguished Service Medal — the only Englishman ever to receive this honour.

The next appointment came after the war when, as Secretary of State for War, Churchill was given the daunting task of demobilising millions of servicemen from Europe and the East to Britain.

He had proved himself a very able international communicator during the Great War. He had been, as ever, controversial and forthright, but nevertheless admired, respected and honoured.

The years that were to follow before World War Two are Churchill's 'middle years', spent as an able, prominent and active (though often depressed) politician.

CHAPTER TWO
The Middle Years

Churchill held the Office of Secretary of State for the Colonies until 1922 when, at the General Election, he lost his seat. This is bound to happen in a democratic system where voters change their minds, but Churchill proceeded to lose a further three elections over two years. He fought his way back to Parliament as a Constitutionalist with Conservative support for Woodford, Essex in 1924. Soon after his return to Parliament Churchill rejoined the Conservatives and the Prime Minister, Stanley Baldwin, made him Chancellor of the Exchequer.

This was a major Cabinet post, but like so many politicians, now, as then, he found that oratorical prowess in regard to the economy is nothing in the face of reality. Sticking to orthodox economic policies, failing to take account of the damage done to the British economy during the First World War and ignoring the increasing competitiveness of the rest of the industrialised world, Churchill failed to put the ailing British economy to rights — if anything he exacerbated the problem.

He returned Britain to the gold standard that had stood between Britain and the rest of the world before the outbreak of World War One. With the falling wages that this entailed and the longer hours that people were required to work, the result was economic recession and, initially, strikes. Of these strikes the General Strike of 1926 is the most famous, though this was short lived. Churchill became unpopular throughout this period though, as his reputation for being a warmongerer increased. This was fuelled by his aggressive stance on the General Strike; he wanted to call in the army, he called the strike 'unconstitutional', and he used propaganda techniques to dispel the threat it posed to capitalism.

On the propaganda front he used, effectively, both radio and the newspapers, publishing a government paper called 'The British Gazette' daily throughout the eight day strike.

Despite the early set-backs, Churchill persevered, being caricatured as a no-nonsense Chancellor and also as a bricklayer (a hobby he was known to have pursued for 'relaxation'). He was also still to be found on cigarette cards. John Player and Sons presented him as Chancellor in 'Straight Line Caricatures' of 1926. The same year, Turf Cigarettes, in their series, 'Famous Escapes', recalled his daring escape from the Boers in Pretoria a quarter of a century before.

It was through his Chancellorship that Churchill was first depicted as a toby jug — by Goss China in 1927. Churchill imposed a new tax on betting in 1926, which was, not surprisingly, unpopular and the toby jug portrays him with cherubic features, seated, wearing a blue coat (sometimes green), with hands together as though in prayer. The inscription on the top hat is, 'Any Odds Bar One', (a humorous reference to the Betting Tax) 'That's Me Who Kissed the Blarney Stone'. This is one of the very few ceramic items concerning Churchill that were introduced between the wars.

By 1929 the Conservative government and its economic policies were so unpopular that a Labour Government was voted in for the first time. Although Britain came off the gold standard, the policies of the new Labour Government were not very radical, indicating that to some extent, Churchill's failure as a Chancellor was a result of old ideas and few new options.

In spite of the criticisms, Churchill was still held, in 1929, to be 'the greatest rhetorician in Parliament' in a cigarette card issue by Carreras in 1929 and in 1930 as, 'One of the most brilliant writers of the day'. In 1932, a Godfrey Phillips card in the series, 'Personalities of Today' lists his outstanding achievements and books.

However, the thirties must be seen as the wilderness years for Churchill. Even when the Conservatives formed a Government he was left on the back-benches without ministerial office. He was considered too controversial, too erratic, impetuous and provocative. He could even be considered too old, already having had a distinguished and historic role behind him and now, in 1934, approaching sixty years of age.

In the 1930's Churchill's attention was drawn to international events — particularly the re-armament of Germany under a Fascist regime. He, more than any other politician, warned of the looming dangers to peace and democracy. Fellow Members of Parliament treated Churchill's words with scepticism and even when Churchill revealed the massive spending by Germany on arms in 1937, the Prime Minister of the day, Neville Chamberlain, insisted that the spending was not excessive.

Having no ministerial burden during the thirties, Churchill devoted much of his spare time to writing, as well as to his brick-building and painting. This latter hobby was taken up late in his years, but he considered it very theraputic and proved to have considerable aptitude.

Churchill was the author of many newspaper articles and was able to complete the massive and highly acclaimed biography of his famous ancestor, John Churchill, First Duke of Marlborough. The Duke was born in 1650 and was one of the greatest masters of war in British history. He was promoted to Dukedom in 1702 and won the Battle of Blenheim against the French and Bavarians in 1704. One of the rewards reaped by the Duke for his illustrious and successful military career was Blenheim Palace itself, the birthplace of Winston. The research for his biography took Churchill and his assistants six years to complete.

Churchill's literary output during the 1930's extended further, with an autobiographical account of 'My Early Life' up to 1908, 'Great Contemporaries', 'Step by Step', 'Thoughts and Adventures', the fifth volume of 'World Crisis' and also a one volume edition of 'World Crisis'.

In 1935 a set of cigarette cards entitled, 'In the Public Eye', this time by Godfrey Phillips, gave details of the various offices Churchill had held throughout his life, and the last card of all was in an Ardath Tobacco set of 1937 called, 'Empire Personalities', in which he was said to be one of the most vivid personalities in Parliament.

The storm clouds gathering over Europe darkened when Hitler took the first steps toward achieving German aims and in 1936 ordered his troops to march into and occupy the Rhineland. This was followed two years later by the annexation of Austria. With growing truculence Hitler next agitated for the Sudentenland in Czechoslovakia where there lived a large German speaking population.

Churchill's fears and many warnings were to prove well-founded. In spite of repeated attempts by Chamberlain to make peace with Hitler before he went too far, the Germans occupied Czechoslovakia. Britain had promised Poland — next on Hitler's list — that it could be assured of military support should it be attacked, and in August 1939, when German troops massed along the Polish frontier, Chamberlain issued an ultimatum to Hitler, requesting withdrawal. When a second ultimatum was issued and ignored, with Germany attacking Poland on September 1st, 1939, Britain and France declared war on Germany.

The war had been inevitable since 1934 when Hitler came to power, and Churchill, with full justification, was to call the world war which it spawned, "The needless war".

At almost sixty-five years of age, Churchill was suddenly taken from the shadows and placed in command of the Admiralty, again as First Lord. His finest years were not behind him — they were still to come. This is tellingly portrayed by pictures taken that year in 1939. Churchill appears to be elderly and semi-retired early in the year, but upon his reappointment, at the steps of the Admiralty, he has lost ten years and his face clearly shows the joy he must have felt at the news. This has provided the inspiration for a plate by Kevin Francis Ceramics, who, fifty years on have commissioned a painting of Churchill as he appeared at that time. This plate depicts Churchill in his study, with the exuberence of his new office clearly radiating from him.

Churchill's return to the Admiralty after twenty-five years was greeted with relief and enthusiasm by his colleagues in Parliament, and the people of Britain, particularly the press. In the new mood for fighting, the spirit which had held back Churchill from office was to be harnessed by the people as a major threat to the advance of German troops and Fascism the world over.

The Admiralty, pleased to have him back, flashed to the whole fleet the signal, "Winston is back": and back he was.

Churchill's enormous and immediate popularity was reflected in the number of commemorative items which appeared around that date — in unprecedented and fascinating numbers. Pieces produced early on in the war emphasised his naval connection, among them an ashtray by L.M.C. of London who, with considerable imagination, made a figurine of the First Lord, bemedalled, dressed like an Admiral standing buoyantly on the edge of the tray. The pose reflects a joyous Churchill, joyous at his return to the fleet after the popular clamour for his reinstatement. He certainly looks impressive, with his Trinity House Dress, a telescope under his left arm, cigar in right hand and a fierce bulldog by his side. This rare item is inscribed on the front, 'The Star Turn' — Churchill having referred to himself in his autobiography as a 'Star Turn' at his election campaign in Oldham in 1900.

This very rare souvenir is believed to be the first piece which associates Churchill with a bulldog — the animal to which he, and indeed the whole British nation, was associated.

Another ornamental figure (unmarked) forms part of a series of early war leaders, including Chamberlain and Lord Gort. This features him in a double-breasted jacket, a yachting cap in his hand while he stands in the pose of a colossus over the helm of a cruising warship.

The theme is continued with a large character jug of Churchill as he looks sternly towards his enemy. In this Shorter and Son piece an anchor forms the handle, again of naval significance, and the jug itself is brightly coloured, his hair being a rather stark (though very erronous) black. The better coloured of these jugs are marked 'Fielding'.

Another piece from this period is a plain, cream coloured mask-jug which presents a sphinx like Churchill which has a remarkable likeness about it. The vessel itself is about eight inches high and has a curious scroll-like decoration around the sides and front, presumably to represent the waves of the sea. The immediate impression is of a ship's figurehead, this almost certainly being the artist's intention. It is marked underneath, 'Kirkland, Etruria'.

During the early war months several satirical medallions were struck in Germany. All were designed by Guido Goertz and cast by Karl and Guido Goertz of Munich. The first commemorated the sinking of the liner, 'Athenia' just a few hours after war was declared. The obverse shows Churchill seated on a wooden crate, with the legend, 'Ein Meister der Luge' (A master of the lie). The reverse design has a skeleton seated astride the bow of the liner holding a bomb with the Union Jack in its left hand. The second medallion announced the sinking of the aircraft carrier, 'Courageous', in September, 1939. On the obverse Neptune rises from the sea holding in its left hand a paper bearing the message, 'Torped Von Deutsch U Boot 18 Sep. 1939'

(Torpedoed by a German U Boat 8 Sept. 1939). The legend, 'Die Hiobsbotschaft an Churchill' (Job's message of bad news to Churchill). The third medallion recorded the sinking of the aircraft carrier, 'Ark Royal'. On the reverse Premier Chamberlain is seated between Churchill, the First Lord of the Admiralty, and Hore-Belisha, Secretary of State for War. Churchill's hand rests on a paper on which is written, 'Deutsche Bomber Gegen brit. See. Streitkrafte, 27 Sep. 1939', (German Bombers against British Naval Forces 27 Sep. 1939). The legend, 'Wie Sag ich Meinen Volke', (How do I tell my people) is on the reverse and a skeleton holds the Union Jack in the waves of the sea as a German bomber flies overhead. The 'Ark Royal' was in fact sunk by torpedo on 13 November, 1941.

CHAPTER THREE
Destiny

Churchill was convinced thoughout his youth that he was treading an ordained path, destined to accomplish great things. He took a giant step nearer this dream when, in May 1940, after a debate in the House of Commons following the withdrawal of British troops in Norway, Chamberlain resigned the Premiership. Although Lord Halifax was preferred by the King and Chamberlain, instatement of him in such a position as Prime Minister would be unconstitutional since no first born son of a Peer can sit in the House of Commons (unless he renounces the title). But there was no doubt in the Commons who the leader should be, and Churchill was invited by H.M. the King at the most critical period in Britain's history, to form a national Government. Churchill wrote about the episode, "That as I went to bed at about 3 a.m. I was conscious of a profound relief, at last I had the authority over the whole scene. I felt as if I were walking with destiny and that all my past life had been but a preparation for this hour and for this trial. My warnings over the past six years had been so numerous, so detailed and now so terribly vindicated that no-one could gainsay me."

He was also Minister of Defence and this twin capacity, combined with his military knowledge, enabled him to deal directly with his military leaders, even dominate them. He was the first Prime Minister to do this.

When Churchill took over as Prime Minister the situation facing Britain was extremely grave. The battle of the Atlantic with the heavy loss of shipping and the consequent danger to Britain's lifeline was a constant worry. Germany had overrun, conquered and occupied Czechoslovakia, Poland, Denmark and Norway. Holland and Belgium were invaded and both near to surrender. On the 14th May, 1940, the Prime Minister read to the Cabinet a message received from M. Reynaud stating that the Germans had broken through at Sedan, that the French were unable to resist the combination of tanks and dive bombers, and asking for ten more squadrons of fighter planes to re-establish the line. In a dramatic telephone call from France on 15th May, Premier Reynauld told Churchill that France was beaten and had lost the battle. In a brave attempt to bolster French morale and keep them fighting, Churchill flew to Paris the next day. He made two more abortive flights to Paris in May still urging them to fight on. Again, on 11th June, even after the British army had been evacuated from Dunkirk, he made yet another very dangerous flight, during which he saw German fighter planes, to France. Most of the French leaders whom he met were now infected with a mood of dejection and defeatism and wanted to surrender to avoid further loss of life and damage to property. Despite all Churchill's exhortations and assurances that Britain would fight on, France succumbed and on 22 June accepted Hitler's Armistice terms. Britain was now alone in the fight for freedom, nothing stood between Britain and the might of Germany except the Channel, the Royal Air Force and Winston Churchill.

In preparation for the expected invasion the Premier spent much time touring coastal defences, meeting troops, checking on the state of readiness and always paying attention to raising morale. In a speech on 18 June he referred to the colossal disaster in France, then looked forward to the exploits of our fighter pilots, "This brilliant youth who would have the glory of saving their native land". The confidence which he placed in them was fully justified, for in July, the Battle of Britain began. The German planes first attacked shipping in the Channel and harbours, then mounted ferocious attacks on airfields and installations. In August great daily air battles raged over southern England as the Luftwaffe made an all out effort to smash the Royal Air Force. The fighting reached its greatest intensity in mid-September, but by then the German Air Force had suffered very heavy losses and Britain lived to fight on. Churchill paid tribute to the gallant British and Allied fighter pilots, "...Never in the field of human conflict was so much owed by so many to so few..."

Suddenly the Luftwaffe abandoned its attempt to destroy the Royal Air Force and turned its attention to terrorising cities by massed forces of bombers. Churchill was ever conscious of raising morale and toured the bombed and devasted areas of cities — being held in great affection by the people. He symbolised the British spirit and was clearly an outstanding example to his fellow countrymen, providing true and dogged determination against a force far more mighty than our own and he succeeded in uniting the people of Britain as no other man had done.

The regard and indeed admiration in which he was held influenced many ceramic firms to make toby jugs in his image. These would serve the purpose of bringing a likeness of the great man into the homes of many British people and inspiring them in the daily struggle for victory. He was an ideal subject for this typically British method of portrayal and indeed the series which emerged was remarkable for the many facets of Churchill which they explored. Never had so many variants of these jugs been made to feature one individual man, and none have been made on such a scale since. They are of great historical importance and indicate the degree to which he was idolised by his countrymen during the tense and anxious war years.

Churchill is seen in the image which each artist wished to portray, many of them with considerable charm, wit and imagination. The following examples, by no means exhaustive, show how the picture we have of Winston Churchill developed. The reader must bear in mind at this point that such an image was closely in keeping with the character of the British people as well, and not just for Churchill himself, for in other societies he may have been portrayed as a demi-god, a dictator, a saint, or indeed he may have fallen victim to a power struggle and never emeged as Britain's wartime leader. In that Churchill was represented in these forms is as much due to the strength and courage of the British nation as to the virtues of Churchill himself.

Winston Churchill was looked upon by many people as the incarnation of John Bull and, as the war progressed, this likeness became more and more apparent. Strong, firm, determined features, a pugnacious face, his sturdy, ample figure and fierce patriotism, all combined to convey the impression of utter reliability and solidity that is commensurate with the legendary character of John Bull. All that was missing was the Union Jack waistcoat. Churchill's striking resemblance to John Bull is superbly captured in a toby jug modelled by E. T. Baily, produced by Burgess and Leigh and issued in 1940, primarily for export to the United States of America. He is dressed in red hunting coat and black hat, standing with legs astride, with an alert bulldog standing guard beneath him. Both look defiant and ready to face any challenge. The sides and back of the jug have much interesting detail moulded into the design and include a tank, plane, anti-aircraft gun and an anchor set against a Union Jack background. The jug is aptly entitled, 'Bulldogs' and on the base is impressed the famous quotation, "We shall defend every village, every town, every city." A further impression reads, 'John Bull Churchill'. As a result of paintresses being transferred to munitions or other warwork, some of these jugs were issued without colour. Ernest Bailey, the creator of the jug, based its design on the John Bull stance, and his intention was to convey the aggressive vigour of Churchill whom he greatly admired.

There were many attributes about Churchill upon which the artist or modeller could seize and exaggerate. These 'gifts' to the caricaturists were eagerly accepted and delightfully emphasised by them. There was the bow tie, usually of spotted pattern, the range of hats, Homburg, Cambridge, top hat and trilby. Also, with the hat of the Royal Yacht Squadron, set at a jaunty angle, he wore the double breasted blue jacket which gave him a distinct nautical appearance, one which he much favoured. Then there was the collection of ceremonial dress — the Privy Councillor's uniform, the uniform of the Lord Warden and Admiral of the Cinque Ports, the Trinity House dress, the Army and Air Force uniforms. From this impressive wardrobe he loved to select as the occasion demanded.

He was particularly fond of siren suits, unique one piece garments like tailored boiler suits of velvet which he designed himself. One of these suits was usually worn at home, either when working or relaxing. Finally there was the walking stick which he loved to brandish and, of course, the inevitable cigar, either clamped firmly in the teeth or held in the hand. He was the most photographed and quoted of men, and the artist could, besides choosing from a wealth of well-known expressions, select a suitable quotation to embellish the work. Churchill's armoury of words thus aided the creation of the image he was to become.

One of the first character jugs made during his Premiership was designed by C. J. Noke for Doulton, issued in 1940. This was a large, all white, two-handled jug which was not considered a good likeness and to which Churchill himself is supposed to have taken a dislike. Probably because of this it had only a short period of availability, being withdrawn within one year. Royal Doulton are noted for the excellence which they bring to pottery and china, and the jug itself, being a rare item, will fetch over £5,000 today at auction. Collecting fever, the subject matter, the design, rarity and quality of production combine to make this such a valuable item. Yet it is so inconspicuous in its composition that a number of these will inevitably reside in the homes of unwitting families throughout Britain, America, Australia, New Zealand and South Africa. Two known colour versions of this jug have been uncovered and are considered unpriceable.

The year 1941 began with Britain at bay, still alone, still holding out defiantly against overwhelming odds, much against the expectations of the whole world. Churchill was now firmly entrenched as the nation's fighting premier and spokesman. A plate published by Crown Ducal entitled, 'Britain's Fighting Premier,' displays a photograph by Cecil Beaton which shows Churchill seated at his desk. He was now firmly held in the hearts of British people as the inspiration of the greatest hopes, and the applause and cheers were out, 'Good old Winnie'.

More manufacturers joined in this acclamation by introducing their own tribute to Churchill and in that year, 1941, many more jugs made their appearance. From Minton came a white china character jug of the Premier with a rather serene expression under a peaked yachting cap. The portrait detail of this jug by Eric Owen is extremely good, and it is a great pity that a shortage of materials did not permit the colouring of this jug as it would look splendid in full colour. A matching companion to this was produced of President Roosevelt. Minton also issued at the same time a china head of Churchill by Eric Owen, but again, unfortunately a shortage of materials prevented colouring it, which would have undoubtedly enhanced its already fine appearance. A very stern head and shoulder jug of the Prime Minister, perhaps reflecting the grim days of 1941 came from the Meakins factory, modelled appropriately by Frank Potts. This Homburg hatted jug was issued in two sizes and was available in either a single colour or all white. A second jug, this time a toby, was introduced by Kirklands, depicting a dignified Churchill, seated, leaning forward and grasping his left coat lapel whilst smoking a cigar, which is held in the right hand. Churchill is in sombre, formal morning dress, his top hat detachable, the mood being one of resolve in face of threat of traditional values and ways of life in Britain. There is also a character jug of Churchill made in two sizes by Cooper Clayton showing a rather squashed faced Premier wearing a trilby hat, cigar edged firmly in the mouth and the handle shaped like an umbrella.

Thorley offered two good examples, one of Churchill with Homburg hat, cigar in mouth and, for a handle, a flagpole with the Union Jack flying aloft. The second jug was a small, very original toby of a seated Churchill, dressed as a naval man, bottle in hand, preparing to pour a drink in a glass held in the other hand. This is Churchill being portrayed in a typical pose of 'The Drinking Toby' and more clearly identifies him with the earliest of British Toby jugs. The handle, more unusually, is a yellow lion rempant, the Red Ensign being draped over the back of the chair. This fine, well coloured toby, is entitled 'The Captain,' which appears on the base. Two contrasting head and shoulder jugs came from Wilton Pottery, one depicting Churchill in a blue jacket and yachting cap, the other showing him attired in morning dress, with top hat and cigar in the mouth. The latter vessel was also issued in an uncoloured version without cigar. Both jugs have the same inscription on the base, 'Never was so much owed'.

Following their withdrawn item, Doulton brought out another Churchill jug in 1941. This one was a full figure toby of the Prime Minister, seated, wearing an overcoat and the favoured homburg hat, gloves in hand, holding a walking stick and with a cigar held in his mouth. The artist on this occasion was H. Fenton and it was very well received, being a much better likeness than their previous offering. It has become so popular that it must be one of the most familiar toby jugs ever produced. it is still in production and continues to be one of Royal Doulton's best selling tobies, an incredible record which testifies to the attractive design and the lasting admiration for the subject matter. This jug was almost certainly introduced before Churchill had instituted the famous 'V' campaign in August, 1941, and it is interesting to speculate whether the artist would have had Churchill making the 'V' had it been modelled a few months later. If we ask why the jug has been so popular, even today, the answer in part must be the now entrenched identification of Winston Churchill with the most typical of art-ceramic forms in British history. The fact that Churchill is not making the famous V sign probably makes the image more lasting, since the action stirred the hearts of the people during the war years, but it is as revered statesman that he is most appropriately depicted. There is a certain elderly kindness in the poise and facial contours of the jug creating an image of Churchill which endures the decades. The jug is available in three sizes and the early versions have 'Winston Churchill Prime Minister of Great Britain 1940,' inscribed on the base.

Proclaiming the defiant and unconquerable spirit of the war years, some jugs carried a stirring extract from one or other of Churchill's famous speeches. A character jug by E. T. Bailey for Burgess and Leigh presents the Prime Minister in blue jacket, cap and, of course, the beloved cigar in his mouth. On the base is the inscription, "We shall defend every village, every town, every city." It was also supplied in a single colour version and a smaller size. This jug has a similar expression to Ernest Bailey's earlier jug — the John Bull. The dress, however, is different symbolising once more the naval connection even though Churchill was already Prime Minister. A few of these jugs were re-issued in 1965 following the death of Sir Winston, a slight difference being that the handles of these later jugs were coloured brown as opposed to the green on the wartime models.

A handsome patriotic toby modelled by Watkins, made by Beswick, shows Churchill sitting on a Union Jack covered chair, holding before him an open scroll on which is proclaimed, "We shall fight on the beaches, on the landing grounds, in the fields and in the hills. We shall never surrender." A sculptured Lion rampant forms the handle, representing the spirit of Britain. Another Beswick model introduced in 1941 is a china statuette of the Premier, dressed in his naval type dress, with hat raised aloft in the right hand. The base bears the quotation, "We shall not flag nor fail." An interesting detail is the gas mask case which is hanging on a strap over his left shoulder, serving as a grim reminder of the war years when everybody had to carry a gas mask to protect them against a gas attack. This intriguing figure was created by Owen.

A pair of tobies came from the Spode factory of W. T. Copeland and Sons in 1941. Their artist, Eric Olsen, modelled these jugs; one being Churchill sitting, deep in thought, dressed in blue coat, trilby hat, yellow waistcoat and bow tie. The hands are clasped and there is the customary cigar in his mouth. The other jug, which matches, is of President Roosevelt. This charming pair have an unusual square appearance and some uncoloured examples were produced. The Anglo-American partnership is represented by these jugs, thereby recognising the role that America was to play in the liberation of Europe.

Olsen and Spode combined to produce a standing portrait figure of Churchill in bone china, wearing a black coat, pinstriped trousers and homburg hat. His left hand, holding gloves, is raised as if acknowledging the crowds while the right hand holds the cigar. This superior statuette was also made in fine earthenware. A few of the earthenware figures, were reissued in 1965 as memorial pieces, the only other difference being that there were no pinstripes on the trousers.

Another attractive item from Spode was a large white jug, this time not a toby, which carries on the front a central portrait of Churchill beneath a diving hurricane fighter plane. Flanking the Premier's solemn face is a battleship to the right and a tank to the left, representing the three fighting forces on land, sea and air. Above the scene in a semi-circle is the quotation, "All I can offer is blood, tears, toil and sweat". Below, within a scroll, is another quotation, "Never in the field of human conflict was so much owed by so many to so few." The reverse of the jug carries a very patriotic design: a bulldog sits on the Union Jack which covers most of the northern hemisphere of the globe. Above the globe is a further quotation, "Give us the tools and we will finish the job." Below, again within a scroll is the verse from Longfellow's, 'Building of the Ship':

"Sail on, O ship of State,
Sail on, O Union, strong and great,
Humanity with all its fears,
With all the hopes of future years,
is hanging on thy fate."

This was quoted by President Roosevelt in his letter to Churchill of 20 January, 1941.

This sombre, telling jug truly captures and conveys to the beholder the tense mood of the anxious days of its manufacture. There were some variations to the finish of this particular piece, some with the printing in brown, others with the printing in black while some were hand-coloured on glaze. The reverse design also varied, some having only the Union Jack. The bulldog with Union Jack design was used on some ashtrays. Other ashtrays carried the solemn portrait of Churchill.

Churchill was ever a buoyant optimist and never lost an opportunity even in the darkest war days when news was at its blackest, to encourage people. His very presence with his fingers raised in the victory salute acted like a tonic on his war weary countrymen. The 'V' for Victory campaign was introduced in August, 1941 and this morale boosting theme was successfully worked into many souvenirs.

This gesture, as the war years continued, became the salute of defiance adopted by the civilians and servicemen of Britain and also by members of the Resistance in Nazi-occupied Europe. It was to become as much a part of the Churchillian image as his Havana cigars and he was rarely photographed without making the salute.

Churchill had appreciated the necessity and importance for morale of a bold gesture and he had persisted when appropriate in giving the salute from his early days as Prime Minister in 1940. Initially, the media did not appreciate its significance until an incident in August 1941, when Churchill was addressing reporters as he left for a summit meeting with President Roosevelt in Newfoundland. A 'Daily Express' photographer recorded it on film on what is thought to be the first occasion. The caption read, "The 'V' sign — this novel salute made by the Prime Minister at the conclusion of his interview . . .

having stressed that Hitler and Nazism would be defeated and the Allies victorious . . .". The gesture was made to illustrate his determination and from that time forward a Churchillian legend has been established.

The origins of the sign, however, are not new. It took its rise over 500 years before when the archers of the English Army at the Battle of Agincourt made the gesture to their opponents in the French Army. The archer uses the index and middle fingers of the drawing hand to pull back the bow string, it being almost impossible to fire a bow using any other hold. At the time of Agincourt the troops of the French army had been ordered to cut off the bow fingers of every Englishman they captured and as an act of defiance at the commencement of the battle, the King's archers raised the index and second fingers to show scant regard for the threats of the French army. Although greatly outnumbered, the English under Henry V won what is still regarded as one of the greatest battles in history against overwhelming odds.

Forgotten, the salute of defiance had passed into obscurity in the annals of history but Winston Churchill was aware of its meaning and existence and he revived the salute as an act of defiance and created with it the symbol of the letter 'V' for Victory.

A third jug from Burgess and Leigh, again by Bailey, has the Prime Minister seated, in formal dress, with a very thoughtful expression. The crooked left arm forms the handle of the jug while the fingers are held in the 'V' sign. The morse code for the letter 'V', which was used by the BBC to introduce programmes to Europe during the war, is impressed on the front of the jug. This jug makes up three jugs produced by Burgess and Leigh during the war years; a very likeable trio which is exceptional, since other potteries did not produce more than two.

A coloured earthenware bust signed, "J. Edge," dated August, 1941 of unknown manufacture, displays a large 'V' prominently in the front. The date on this bust indicates that it was made very soon after Churchill had introduced the sign and it further indicated the immediate success with which it was met. The bust does not, however, bear a good likeness of the Premier. A naval type portrait of Churchill making the 'V' sign was woven in Macclesfield silk and was possibly made for use as a cushion cover.

Britain's grim year of fighting alone the axis powers was ended in June, 1941 when Hitler attacked the USSR. Churchill immediately pledged all help possible to the new and mighty ally.

Early in September, 1939, Churchill was delighted to receive a letter from President Roosevelt expressing pleasure at Churchill's return to the Admiralty and that he would welcome being kept in touch personally. Churchill replied, signing himself, 'Former Naval Person'. This exchange of letters laid the foundation of a lasting friendship and strengthened the Anglo-American partnership leading to a flood of vital aid from America. Churchill ensured that America was fully aware of Britain's desperate need for a large stockade of armaments, munitions and other essential supplies. He found in the President a most concerned and generous friend, eager to be kept fully informed of all aspects of Britain's struggle and willing to give all help possible. Before the Lease Lend Act was drawn up and signed, Churchill had already negotiated with the President for the transfer of 250,000 rifles and 50 destroyers from America to Britain. A speech by Churchill on 9 February, 1941 concluded with the challenging appeal, "Give us the tools and we will finish the job." This unique and historic request was commemorated by Wedgwood, who in 1941 produced a glazed blue tankard with those words circumscribed round the bottom. The tankard was designed by Arnold Machin and has an applied cameo of Churchill in white complete with cigar in mouth. This is one of the few souvenirs showing Churchill wearing an ordinary tie. A lion rampant on the opposite side completes the decoration. Shortly after, Wedgwood issued a matching tankard with the President's profile on one side and the American Eagle on the other.

In August, 1941 one of the Royal Navy's latest battleships, H.M.S. 'Prince of Wales', with Churchill on board, sailed stealthily from Scapa Flow to a secret rendezvous with the U.S.S. 'Augusta'. After a perilous crossing of the U-boat infested Atlantic Ocean, the battleship anchored by the awaiting American cruiser in the Bay of Placentia. On board the U.S.S. 'Augusta' was the President of the United States. Here in this bay, just off the coast of Newfoundland, the two leaders held the first in a series of remarkable wartime meetings. They visited each other's ship, conferred on the state of the war, and shared in a church service aboard H.M.S. 'Prince of Wales', and the outcome of their discussions was the drawing up of a joint statement which became known as the 'Atlantic Charter'. This document outlined details of the framework in which the aims and ideals of Britain and America in war and peace were set out.

This historic conference and the Atlantic Charter itself were com-memorated by several manufacturers. A plate was published by Vernon Kilns of America with a pink, all-over transfer and sketched portraits of Roosevelt and Churchill who face each other beneath their respective flags; the poles of which are arranged to form a V for Victory. The warships which bore them to the meeting place, together with quotations from speeches by both leaders are included in the design, "Never was so much owed by so many to so few" by Churchill, and "It must be done, it shall be done, it will be done," by Roosevelt. Also comemmorating this important event was a plate published by Meakins with a design incorporating profiles of the President and Premier opposite each other. The globe, upon which stands the Statue of Liberty is between them. This souvenir bears the words, "Champions of Democracy". The transfer was also used on a small number of beakers.

Churchill was in a buoyant mood during the time on board ship and most photographs taken there show him looking confident, smiling and attired in the familiar double breasted blue jacket and cap. One of the photographs was used by Lancaster as an illustration on plates commemorating the occasion. The picture portrays the President and the Prime Minister seated side by side engaged in conversation. The same illustration is to be found on a small number of ashtrays and dishes. An excellent toby jug of Churchill wearing the above mentioned dress and with a cigar in his mouth dates from the meeting. He is sitting on a ship's chair which is draped with the Union Jack. This exceedingly rare jug bears one of the finest resemblances to Churchill and wonderfully conveys his indomitable spirit, cheerful and resolute in times of greatest peril. It is most unfortunate that there is no clue to the maker's name but it is believed to be by Floral China. The splendid battleship, H.M.S. 'Prince of Wales' was tragically sunk, with much loss of life, off the Malayan coast by the Japanese just four months after the Atlantic meeting.

On hearing of Japan's savage attack on Pearl Harbour, December 1941, Churchill immediately contacted Roosevelt. The very next day arrangements were made for another meeting between them. This took place in America the same month. During his stay in the now allied United States, Churchill accepted an invitation to address both Houses of Congress and was received with great enthusiasm. He then journeyed north to speak to the Canadian Parliament in Ottawa. In recognition of his ceaseless efforts, outstanding leadership and courage, Churchill was awarded the title 'Man of the Year' for 1941 by 'Time' Magazine.

Churchill had been at the helm for eighteen months when the title was given to him. The year 1941 had been one of mixed fortunes, heavy losses of ships in the Atlantic and two of Britain's best battleships, "H.M.S. Prince of Wales" and H.M.S. "Repulse" both sunk. On the other hand Britain now had two mighty allies.

Winston Churchill was appointed Lord Warden and Admiral of the Cinque ports in December 1941 — the first commoner to hold this ancient office. Because of the intense pressure and heavy demands on his time during the war, the installation did not take place until August 1946. He wears the uniform of that Office in a particularly fine jug bearing the 'Clarice Cliff' backstamp. The jug, made by Wilkinsons, shows Churchill sitting on a bulldog draped in the Union Jack. There is some speculation as to whether Clarice Cliff modelled this toby, since she has never been noted for her modelling ability and the figures which do exist are very crude.

Further details in the design show a destroyer cradled in Churchill's arms, the left hand holding the customary cigar. Around the base of the jug is the inscription, 'Going into action and may God defend the Right' — the last five words being taken from his speech to the House of Commons on 11th

September, 1940.

This lovely jug tells us so much about Churchill, his love of uniforms, former Naval connection, fondness for cigars, tenacity, patriotism, supreme confidence and powers of oratory. It was the intention of Wilkinsons to produce a set of toby jugs of military, naval and political men in the fashion of their famous series by F. Carruthers-Gould, made during and just after the First World War. This was the first in the proposed series to have included Chamberlain, Roosevelt, Wavell and Mitchell (the aircraft designer of Spitfire fame). Although a few jugs of all these personalities were made as prototypes, it was not possible to proceed with the series as an embargo was placed on essential materials and a high proportion of the firm's skilled workers were called up to serve in the forces.

The enormous and vital help given by America under the Lease Lend Act engineered by Roosevelt, was received by a needy and grateful Britain. Consequently the President was held in very high esteem and was very popular with the British people. With the entry of America into the war he was now regarded as Churchill's partner, and portraits of both leaders began to appear together on souvenirs. A small bud vase by Royal Winton features sketches of them with the Union Jack and the Stars and Stripes. This transfer was also used on a small range of earthenware including cups and saucers and sweet dishes. A treacle glazed loving cup in the form of a globe was introduced by Royal Victoria Pottery. On the globe are planes and ships in relief which are crossing the Atlantic Ocean from West to East, symbolic of American aid comming to Britain. The handles are represented by standing figures of the President and the Premier. Around the bottom of the cup, again in relief, are the words "Let's drink to Victory, Let's drink to Peace". More souvenirs were made in matching pairs, Royal Winton and C.H. Brannam being among firms who issued jugs of both leaders.

A pair of plates was issued by Soho Pottery, each of which had a central portrait of either Roosevelt or Churchill. A third plate was subsequently issued with a matching portrait of Stalin, which is very rare, thus making an interesting set representing the Grand Alliance.

In January 1942, soon after his return from America, Churchill thought it necessary to ask the Commons for a vote of confidence. This was rather surprising in view of his standing as leader of the allies, but it was to answer critics of the Government and his leadership. Some newspapers had been complaining that not enough was being done to help the Russians and called for a second front to be opened. He won the vote of confidence with the result 464-1. In July the same year he faced a motion of no confidence. The motion was defeated 475-25. With his critics now slammed Churchill was able to get on with the war effort.

Huge sums of money were required to pay for the war and people were constantly being exhorted and persuaded under the slogan "Save for Victory" to invest their money in Government savings schemes. This slogan was impressed on the backs of money boxes made in the form of a bust of the Prime Minister. These boxes were of a composite material and came in a choice of colours, green, gold or more commonly, brown.

With the progression of the war the range of souvenirs widened and the variety of functional and novelty mementos increased, reflecting the degree to which Churchill had become part of everyday life in wartime Britain, and also providing an insight into the social climate of those days. Ashtrays, pencils, playing cards, bottle openers — all carrying an impression or portrait of the Prime Minister, made their appearance. For those people who wanted to display their patriotic sentiments there was a selection of badges and brooches, metal or enamelled, from which to choose. These usually sported a profile or other picture of the Premier, frequently with the Victory V.

Even handkerchiefs were printed as souvenirs. These cloth squares could, because of their size, carry a considerable amount of interesting detail. One handkerchief had a central portrait of Churchill, with representations of the armed forces in the corners and around the border. A bomber, fighter plane, warship, tank and field gun were also splendidly displayed on the handkerchief in full colour.

Another handkerchief of silk has, in the centre, part of a famous picture of Churchill holding a Tommy gun. Flags of the allied nations encircle the Prime Minister and form an inner border. The morse code for letter V (...–) runs continuously around the edge and forms the outer border. Other commemoratives like tea spoons were cast in silver and sold in sets of six. The tops of the spoons were impressed with a profile of Churchill looking right.

As in previous wars, patriotic songs played a very important part in maintaining morale and keeping up the British spirit. One popular sentimental song of the war years was called, "There'll always be an England". Elijah Cotton, under their mark 'B.C.M. Nelson Ware', published some plates with a seascape which included a battleship and a war plane. To the right of the picture is Churchill in grey suit, with cigar, smiling confidently. The title, "There'll always be an England", is printed beneath the scene. This design was applied to plates of various sizes and a few cups and saucers. Another well known song was "Roll out the Barrel". Those words appear in relief on a mug by Royal Victoria Pottery. The figure of Churchill with left hand in pocket and head inclined forms the handle. These mugs were produced in several single colour versions, green, tan, blue and white, being the most common.

A medallion cast in lead in 1942 by the London Stonecraft Co. Ltd. commemorated the Battle of Britain. The medallion was attached to a piece of stone from the bombed House of Commons and issued with a certificate of authentication. Some of these medallions which have a bust of Churchill with cigar, facing left, were set in the centre of stone ashtrays. They were designed by F.J. Halnon and distributed by the British Red Cross and St. John Fund, London, to be sold to benefit certain charities.

The Freedom of the City of London was given to Churchill in 1943 and this event was chosen by the Worshipful Co. of Makers of Playing Cards to be depicted on the back of their annual commemorative pack for that year. The picture on the back of the cards captures the scene at the Guildhall where Churchill received this honour from the Lord Mayor of London. Another pack of playing cards from the same period features Churchill and the now traditional bulldog.

During 1943 Doulton issued their famous Union Jack clad bulldog. One variant in particular epitomises Churchill as it humourously clenches a cigar in the mouth and has a naval cap on it's head.

Churchill was amazingly energetic and willingly and frequently travelled many miles to attend vital meetings with military and political leaders. Some of the journeys accross the Atlantic Ocean were undertaken in such prestigious vessels as H.M.S. Prince of Wales, H.M.S. Duke of York, and S.S. "Queen Mary". Other journeys were very uncomfortable — he once flew in the unheated cabin of a Liberator bomber (the cabin had been converted from the bomb rack and the razor edged draughts cut in through many chinks).

All journeys were accompanied by varying degrees of danger. A civil plane flying from Portugal to London was shot down because a German agent had signalled that Churchill was a passenger on board — a thickset man smoking a cigar had walked up to the plane just before it took off from Lisbon airfield. Everyone on board perished when the plane crashed. Leslie Howard, the well known actor, was among the dead.

From the town of Coimbra, Portugal, during the war came a quite superb porcelain figure of Churchill wearing naval type dress, waving his cap as he strides aong. This piece is reminiscent of the Beswick figure in style and also shows the gas mask container. In addition, another very interesting feature is the steel helmet carried by the Premier. The manufacture of this outstanding piece must be an indication of the admiration felt in Portugal for Churchill.

One of his destinations in 1943 was Teheran where, in November, he met Roosevelt and Stalin and took part in a major conference. About the time of the meeting Bovey Tracey Pottery brought out a set of caricature figurines of the three leaders. The series also included a model of a British soldier.

A quaint figurine was made by St. Joseph's Industries of Chingleput, India for sale as fundraisers. Very interestingly, this odd piece, of a bull necked Churchill with hat, cigar and walking stick, still has the original price in rupees on the base.

In 1944 a horse brass was designed by H. Richards featuring the Prime Minister's bust in profile within a scallop edged border. This ornament was sent to him for his approval. Permission was granted for the design to be issued after the war was over. However, the brass went into production earlier, an example being sent to President Roosevelt in April 1944.

Aluminium Bells were manufactured from shot down German aircraft. The bells bore crude profiles in high relief of Churchill, Roosevelt and Stalin and a V for victory on the handle. They were sold to raise money for the Royal Air Force Benevolent Association. Also cast from aluminium, probably from the same source, were large ashtrays with, in the centre, a standing profile of the Premier's head within a large V. This centrepiece was also adapted for use as a car mascot.

The fast, demanding pace that Churchill set himself continued unabated and from June 1944 to January 1945 he made journeys abroad every month. In November 1944 he was in Paris for the Armistice day parade. This visit was commemorated by the French Mint who struck a medal which also honoured the Liberation. The medal, issued in 1945, was designed by Pierre Turin and portrays a bust of Churchill in army uniform looking to the left. The reverse features the Churchill Coat of Arms with, below, a quotation in French from The End of the Beginning speech Churchill had made at the Lord Mayor's Day Luncheon at Mansion House, 10 November 1942, "NOUS N'AVONS QU'UN DESIR VOIR UNE FRANCE FORTE ET LIBRE ENTOUREE DE SON EMPIRE ET REUNIE A L`ALSACE-LORRAINE 10 NOVEMBRE 1942". (For ourselves we have no wish but to see France free and strong, with her Empire gathered round her and with Alsace-Lorraine restored).

With the end of the war in sight and much of formerly occupied Europe now freed, a number of colourful postcards marking the liberation were printed in Belgium. These featured allied leaders, particularly Churchill, in caricature form. One poignant postcard depicts a woman representing Belgium, dressed in red, yellow and black (the national colours), her ankle fetters now broken, giving thanks to Churchill whose face appears Godlike in the sky.

Perhaps surprisingly, there were comparatively few items marking the end of the war. One memento however, was a large medallion struck by John Pinches with, on the obverse, a bust of the Prime Minister facing left and the legend, CHURCHILL. On the reverse a torch of victory is gripped by a hand, the legend, UNFLINCHING, INDOMITABLE, HIS SPIRIT SAVED BRITAIN AND SO THE WORLD. On the field is the inscription, We will fight on land, on sea and in the air until victory is won.

Another victory souvenir was a metal match box cover with portraits of the three allied leaders on one side and the flags of the allies on the opposite side. An accompanying statement reads: Our deepest gratitude to the allies who stood united in defeating the greatest tyrant in history.

After the surrender Churchill proposed that the present Government be maintained until the end of the war with Japan. This was rejected by the Labour M.P.'s. Churchill, therefore, as head of the majority party led a Caretaker Government until the general election. It was three weeks before the result was known — large numbers of votes had to come in from servicemen overseas. Churchill flew home from yet another meeting, this time in Potsdam, on July 26, to hear the result next day. He slept badly and woke with a strong premonition of bad news. His fear was confirmed when the results started to come in. The Labour party had won by a huge majority.

Thus ended the greatest and most inspired term ever served by any Prime Minister.

CHAPTER FOUR
THE AUTUMN YEARS

From being at the centre of things for five years Churchill now felt hurt at what he felt to be a cruel rejection, but he accepted the will of the people, hopeful that in the future he would serve again as Prime Minister. In the New Year's Honours List, published January 1946, it was announced that the King had conferred on Churchill the Order of Merit, the highest honour in the gift of the Crown which does not confer any title on the beholder (he had previously declined the offer of a title, no doubt with a future term as Premier in mind).

The investiture took place on 8th January and some finely moulded plastic busts were issued, with surprisingly fine detail, depicting Churchill wearing the ribbon and insignia of the Order of Merit.

During his years in opposition he was regarded as a major statesman throughout the world and his speeches continued to attract much attention. In March, 1946 Churchill spoke at Westminster College, Fulton, Missouri and pointed out the threat to liberty and peace involved in Russia's establishment of the 'iron curtain', a phrase which is so apt that it is immediately used in any reference to the Berlin Wall. He visited Holland the following May and addressed both Houses of the States General at the Hague and later that year he made a speech at Zurich University advocating a United States of Europe.

Much of his time was spent at Chartwell, the home he loved, where he painted, fed goldfish or laid bricks. There was now time to continue writing and he commenced work on his war memoirs. When this work, in six volumes, was published between 1948 and 1954 it was acclaimed as a masterpiece of history and literature.

His artistic talent was acknowledged when in 1948 he was made Hon. R.A. Extraordinary, and at this time he was fittingly portrayed in a toby jug as an artist!

The jug, by Leonard Jarvis, was made in the traditional style of the first Tobies made by Astbury and Ralph Wood, using similar glazes. In keeping with the old methods used, Churchill wears 18th century dress, a square tailed coat, knee breeches, stockings, shoes with buckles and a three cornered hat. The hair is shoulder length. This remarkable jug with its excellent facial likeness encompasses his talents and pastimes. A trowel is by his right foot, a book, inkwell and quill pen by the other foot. A pallet and brushes are held in the left hand whilst the right hand has the fingers raised in the famous V sign. Not many of these wonderful jugs were made.

The Conservatives were returned to power in 1951 and Winston Churchill became Prime Minister for the second time. He was then almost 77 years of age. No flood of souvenirs accompanied this accession, but some of the items that appeared now reflected his advanced years. A number of plaster type figurenes in several sizes were made in which he is featured as a stout man in various attitudes — hands in pockets or grasping lapels. They are unmarked by the manufacturer and are somewhat crude in style but in spite of this they are very good caricature pieces. Functional and novelty items also arrived on the market, egg cups in the form of the premier's head and candle holders in different sizes. A character jug in bone china of the Premier in peaked cap and white coat came from Arthur Bowyer, and miniature character jugs were made by Snell Ware and Norton China.

In 1953 Churchill was created Knight of the Garter and a plaster figure was produced of him wearing the Sash of the Garter. Later that year he was awarded the Nobel Prize for Literature. This was for his mastery of historical and biographical description as well as for brilliant oratory in defending exalted human values. His 80th birthday was celebrated in Office and he became only the third man in Parliamentary history, (Palmerston and Gladstone were the others), to hold office beyond that age. A bronze medallion was struck by Birmingham Mint marking the anniversary.

By 1955 Churchill was feeling the weight of his years and resigned the Premiership on health grounds, though he remained a member of Parliament for Woodford, Essex.

Jon Douglas modelled several waist length busts, some to serve as book-ends. They were cream coloured, a really good likeness and dated 1955. The Worshipful Company of Makers of Playing Cards again decided on a Churchill theme for their commemorative pack for 1955. The design on the back of the cards includes a portrait of Churchill wearing the Sash of the Order of the Garter and the Ribbon and Insignia of the Order of Merit with the Houses of Parliament providing a background.

Sir Winston Churchill had become the world's greatest elder statesman, respected, admired, beloved and honoured in all free countries. He had been given awards and honours from many nations and during the last decade of his life continued to receive tributes from grateful countries. In October 1955 he was given the Freedom Award, conferred on him by Freedom House, New York, "... For devotion to liberty, courage in adversity, leadership in victory...".

Churchill was the first non-American to be given this award. The following week he was the recipient of another American honour — The Williamsburg Award, ... For services to liberty and justice ... In April, 1963, the United States Congress resolved to offer Churchill the Honorary Citizenship of the U.S.A. This greatest honour had only once before in American history been given to any man. A memorial medal designed by C. M. Castro, struck by Wendell's of Minneapolis in 1965, shows on the obverse a bust of Churchill, and on the reverse Britannia seated with two supporting shields, the Union Jack on one, the American flag on the other with the legend, Friend and Honorary Citizen of the United States.

In 1965 the whole world mourned at Churchill's death, three weeks after he had suffered a massive stroke.

Among the souvenirs which were made to record this sad occasion was a covered urn of unique shape by Spode, richly decorated with crimson and embellished with gilding, bearing his portrait within the belt of the Order of the Garter surmounted by the Churchill family crests and mottos. The reverse contained an extract from one of his famous wartime speeches.

The urn was limited to 125 pieces and a plate with matching design was published by Spode in 1967. Wedgwood manufactured a memorial pint tankard showing Sir Winston against a Chartwell background, his signature on the base. A commemorative crown was struck by the Royal Mint -- the first occasion since Oliver Cromwell that a commoner had appeared on an English coin. On the reverse is a bust of Churchill in siren suit looking right, by Oscar Nemon. The obverse has the head of the Queen by Mary Gillick. A Riyal coin, similar in size to the crown, was struck by the French Mint in Paris for the Kingdom of Yemen.

The British Post Office, British Colonies and many countries printed postage stamps featuring Churchill in a wide variety of portraits and scenes from his life. Many medallions were issued in gold, silver and bronze throughout the world.

Chartwell, the home loved and made famous by Churchill.

CHAPTER FIVE
REMEMBRANCES

In the wake of his passing, manufacturers continued to devise and produce interesting souvenirs. In 1968 B.E.L. products of Birmingham cast a brass door knocker of Churchill with dates of his birth and death and the Houses of Parliament worked into the design. This foundry also cast a bust in the same year. A silver egg spoon with a profile of Sir Winston smoking a cigar impressed at the top of the handle was made by Turner, Simpson in 1968.

The centenary of Churchill's birth, in 1974, was extensively and lavishly commemorated with some of the finest and most expensive souvenirs and ornaments.

Of special interest is the centenary collection of sterling silver created by Garrard, comprising ten items including a punch bowl and ladle with eight cups, a wine jug with six goblets, a statuette and a decanter. A major decorative theme used in this collection is a series of contrasting designs recalling Sir Winston's long and remarkable life. From Coalport came a splendid vase with a hand painted panel of Blenheim Palace on the front signed by a Coalport artist. The reverse has facing profiles of Sir Winston and his coat of Arms surrounded by oak leaves and acorns, symbolising of his determination and character. The vase is twelve inches high and has gold applied to the pedestal base and entwining handles. The cover is surmounted by a gold eagle.

Royal Doulton introduced a black basalt bust on a wooden plinth, with the name and dates of birth and death of Churchill inscribed in gold. Another bust made in the unusual medium of crystal was modelled by Eric Griffiths, who also signed every piece in the edition of 250. The manufacturer of this desirable work of art was Webb, Corbett. Paragon China published a non-portrait plate with the Churchill Coat of Arms in the centre and gothic script in gold around the edge recording his name and date of birth. This firm made a cigar box with matching design, and both of these were a limited edition. A commemorative crown piece was struck by Pobjoy Mint for the Isle of Man Treasury, with silver and cupro nickel examples available. On this occasion postage stamps were printed by Britain and many countries as a tribute to his memory. Many medallions were struck, in a variety of metals, by firms in Britain and throughout the world.

One would have thought that with the magnificent array of items of all sorts issued for the centenary, the commemorative story would be more or less complete but fresh items still emerge. In 1975 a bronze figure of Sir Winston in all the finery of his Garter Robes was sculptured by Karin Churchill, (no relation). The issue of this majestic statuette was limited to 400 pieces. The 40th anniversary of the day Churchill first became Prime Minister was recorded on a silver polished pewter tankard commissioned by the Naval and Military Academy. It bears in high relief a Churchill medallion used on the crown issued by the Royal Mint, 1965. Outstanding details of his life are inscribed on the sides of the tankard. The Pride of Britain series of character jugs by Wood & Sons included one of Churchill, made in 1980. Highland Fine China commemorated the 40th anniversary of the Battle of Britain with a plate containing a central sketch of Churchill. Other items dating from about 1980 include a tiny silver bust to be worn as a charm, carved wooden smoking pipes from France, whisky container, thimbles, and two dolls from Peggy Nisbet. One of the dolls is of Churchill in morning dress, the other is of him in Garter Robes. From Capo di Monte of Italy came a really superb figure of Churchill seated in an armchair, designed by Bruno Merli.

In recent years some well executed statuettes and busts of Churchill have been made in the comparatively new medium of cold cast bronze. These include small replicas of the statue by Ivor Roberts-Jones in Parliament Square, and the statue by Franta Belsky at the Churchill Memorial and Library, Westminster College, Fulton, Missouri. This sculptor was also the creator of a commissioned bust of Churchill cast in 1976, limited to 300 pieces. The television series "The Wilderness Years" screened in the early 1980's was the inspiration for a very fine statuette in cold cast bronze by Keith Lee. This sculpture portrays Churchill in overcoat, hat, carrying gloves and a cigar in mouth, as he appeared in the 1930's. The edition was small, only 250 pieces being cast. A recent addition to Doulton's current range is an earthenware portrait figure of Churchill in white tropical suit, white shoes and white hat. He sports a pink carnation in his buttonhole and carries a walking stick. Modelled by Adrian Hughes and released to coincide with the 40th anniversary of the end of the war, this item is in much demand.

To commemorate the fortieth anniversary of the victory in Europe, The History in Porcelain Company commissioned what is without doubt one of the finest ceramic studies ever produced of Sir Winston Churchill. This recent figure is entitled, 'Sir Winston Churchill, 10, Downing Street, June 4th, 1940'. The Prime Minister is portrayed standing on the steps of Number 10 acknowledging the encouragement of the crowd in a defiant stance making with his fingers the legendary V for Victory sign.

The pose evokes the period of the early 1940's and conveys the tense mood which prevailed in wartime Britain. The accuracy of this sculpture has been achieved by diligent research, meticulous and painstaking attention to detail, and outstanding craftsmanship by former Royal Worcester artists. It is totally lifelike in style and appearance. The waistcoat shows the extra button which he favoured and the gold ring, given to him by Lady Churchill, is seen on the third finger of the right hand. The cufflinks have been faithfully reproduced and his favourite gold Albert hangs from the waistcoat.

The bootscraper outside Number 10 was kicked and damaged by a horse in 1926; even this damage has been incorporated into the work. The fine detail extends to the flesh tints and the colour and texture of the clothing are exactly reproduced. The figure required 245 hours of skilled work for completion with 45 hours being spent on the face alone. Much of the detail was painted by artists using single haired brushes. Seven firings were necessary.

The Lady Soames, Sir John Colville, Lord Home (Prime Minister 1963-64) and Lily Friend, who worked on the Chartwell Estate for many years, have all signed a certificate of authenticity stating that it is correct in every detail, appearance and presentation.

The figure, which is in the scale of 1/7, was modelled by Andrew Turner and produced by Ashmor Fine China of Worcester.

Originally, the limit was set at 350 figures but because of the popularity and demand for it by Members of Parliament, an extra 25 pieces were added to the number.

Two ceramic figures of very high quality aroused great interest when they were introduced late in 1988. Both items were by established artists -- Michael Sutty and Peggy Davies.

In his figurine, Michael Stutty has broken away from traditional portrayals of Sir Winston as an elder statesman and chosen instead to present him as a young man proudly wearing the uniform of the 4th Hussars, the regiment to which he was gazetted at the age of 20 years. It is the first serious study of the uniformed Churchill, which is surprising when one considers his love of uniforms. The detail is superb with the dark, navy blue tunic embellished with gold braid contrasting with the black busby which supports the deep pink plume. From his left side hangs the crested sabretache and sword, black riding boots completing the impressive uniform.

The pose is defiant and shows him standing with legs astride, hands on hips and with the 'ready for anything' insolent look of youth, particularly associated with the impetuous young Churchill. Michael Sutty has given him a slightly older face so that the figure will be instantly identified rather than the youthful features which were then, at 20 years of age, not particularly remarkable. Further detail of great interest is added by the large chain links which encircle the base, representing the chain of the portcullis, which is the symbol of the House of Commons, and which symbolises Churchill's long Parliamentary career. The figure is about 15 inches high.

Peggy Davies is the celebrated former Royal Doulton designer who has a large international following appreciative of her many superb ceramic figures over the years. For her depiction of Sir Winston she has adopted the traditional, typically British Toby Jug. The jug is a most welcome addition to the

44

now famous series of Churchill Tobies. Sir Winston, formally dressed, is seated in a contemplative, sombre mood with, as a companion beside him, the legendary British Lion, reminiscent of Britannia. His left hand rests lightly on the mane of this magnificent beast while the other hand holds his beloved cigar. A volume of Churchill's, 'The History of the English Speaking Peoples,' with the title prominent, rests against his right leg. The back of the figure is draped with the Union Jack and the handle is formed by the flagpole. On the base of this splendid jug, Churchill's famous words are inscribed in Latin: 'The nation had the lion's heart, I provided the roar,' CIVITAS HABUIT LEONIUM ANIMUM EGO FREMITUM PRAEVUI. A further Latin phrase, 'TANTUM MIRABILE EST' (So Much Is Owed) reminds us of the outstanding leadership he provided during the war.

The jug is the first in a high quality series called, 'Spirit of Britain,' featuring great Britons of the twentieth century, issued by Kevin Francis Ceramics Ltd., of Dulwich, London.

Besides the quantity of Churchilliana produced by manufacturers large and small, it is quite a pleasure and a thrill when a unique handmade piece is discovered. Many individual artists and craftsmen attracted and inspired by the stature of Churchill have sought to create their own tribute to him. Some of these 'one-off' items are works of art in their own right and a small selection of such pieces is featured in this survey. These souvenirs include ceramic works and wooden carvings.

Chartwell, the home of the Churchill family from the mid 1920's, is now the most visited National Trust property. Visitors may wander through the mellow house, immerse themselves in the atmosphere and look with fascination at the rooms where Churchill lived, entertained and conferred with leading statesmen and military men from all over the world. The National Trust published a china plate in 1983 in their series commemorating their association with eminent men and women. On this plate, Churchill, clad in smock, is seated at the easel in the garden at Chartwell. The plate by Oakley Fine China was designed by John Holder.

The below ground Cabinet War rooms at Storey Gate, St. James's, London, were opened to the public in 1984. This historic complex of chambers, administered by the Imperial War Museum, has been restored to the early 1940's period and the visitor may, with imagination, be transported back to those tense dramatic war years when Churchill was at the helm and held fast. At Chartwell and Storey Gate there are interesting souvenirs available for purchase.

Of all the many and varied souvenirs and commemorative items, the magnificent and the mundane, the rare and the common, of Sir Winston Churchill it must surely be the superb and fascinating series of toby jugs that hold the pride of place in the hearts of his admirers. These so very English vessels provide a fitting and unique tribute to the life of the greatest English-man.

Well may it be said, "We shall not look upon his like again".

Churchill's grave at Bladon.

THE PUBLIC IMAGES OF CHURCHILL

If a man's greatness may be measured by the number of statues and monuments raised to him then Churchill is the greatest of them all. Statues of Sir Winston stand proud, prominent, and permanent around the world.

It is perhaps more usual for a statue to be erected after the death of the famous person but the first sculptured tributes of Churchill were already being commissioned and even began to appear during the mid 1950's — soon after the end of his second term as Prime Minister. He was, therefore, able to see and appreciate some of the early imposing monuments dedicated to his memory and was present at their unveiling.

Most public statues of Churchill are well known. One of the most familiar is the giant sculpture by Ivor Roberts-Jones in Parliament Square. This magnificent figure stands stooped and brooding in the shadow of Big Ben. Churchill is portrayed with the face of resolution, wearing military greatcoat, his left hand deep in the pocket while the right hand grips the stick upon which he leans. A committee under the chairmanship of Sir John Tilney was set up by Parliament to deal with and commission the statue. The instructions to Ivor Roberts-Jones were for the statue to epitomise the defence of Britain, a figure with the capacity to win his battles, and to symbolise the defiant military mood of Britain at war. A strong sense of the grandeur and greatness of Churchill is evoked in the onlooker who stands before the twelve feet high masterpiece. One has no doubts that the artist has competently captured the unbeaten spirit of Britain in this powerful work. The figure was unveiled by Lady Spencer-Churchill in 1973 in the presence of H.M. The Queen and the Prime Minister, Edward Heath.

Another statue by Ivor Roberts-Jones stands in front of the Index Building, Oslo, Norway. The committee formed to commission the work asked for the same pose as the statue in Parliament Square, which they admired. At first glance this figure, which was erected in 1976, seems to be identical to the London sculpture, although slightly smaller. A closer look however reveals that the mood is completely different. Mr. Roberts-Jones was asked to emphasise 'Churchill The Statesman — Guardian of the Peace,' and in this he has succeeded. The statue, which is nine feet tall, was unveiled by H.M. The King of Norway. A similar figure is privately owned in Sydney, Australia.

There is surely no more fitting site for a memorial figure of a great statesman than by the Arch at the entrance to the House of Commons. Here at the Members' Lobby in the company of former Prime Ministers, Lloyd-George, Balfour, Chamberlain and Disraeli, stands the distinguished leader, head thrust aggressively forward, legs astride, hands on hips, as though delivering a speech. This is the wartime Churchill, the rallying, inspiring, unflagging Premier of the dark war days, encouraging his fellow countrymen in the great battles taking place and those which lay ahead. The characteristic attitude, familiar and frequent to his colleagues, is superbly conveyed by the sculptor, Oscar Nemon. The unveiling of this image, which is seven feet high and weighs one ton, was also carried out by Lady Spencer-Churchill. The Archway above the doors to the House of Commons came from the old House of Commons which was bombed during the war. It was dismantled and re-erected when the new chamber was built and named Churchill Arch by a unanimous decision of the Members of Parliament.

Winston Churchill and Oscar Nemon first met in Marrakesh, North Africa in 1950 and from then on they became firm friends. Naturally this bond presented Nemon with many more opportunities than any other artist to observe, study, and model Churchill. The result is a unique series of bronze busts, heads, and at least eight major statues of Churchill completed over some three decades.

He was commissioned by the Corporation of the City of London in 1954 to sculpture the first full figure statue of Churchill. This work, which may be seen in the Guildhall, is a fine, larger than life seated figure in bronze. The solemn statue of the elder statesman at 80 years of age, is positioned appropriately enough opposite a bronze memorial to the men of the South African Fusiliers who died in the Boer War 1899-1901. He is the sombre presence in that ancient and historic hall and from his raised majestic seat looks silently on at the many important functions which are held there throughout the year.

Pine Gardens, St. Margaret's Bay, Kent is the setting for another Churchill figure by Nemon. This quiet haven near Dover was once in the front line and known as 'Hell-Fire Corner' because of the shelling by the Germans with their long range guns across the Channel during the second world war. The nine feet tall striding giant, depicts an energetic Premier, with head jutting forward and stern determined face and the whole is mounted on an enormous polished black granite plinth. The statue is quite near the beach which may well have been a battlefield had the Germans invaded Britain. It is therefore fitting that the plinth carries in letters of gold the famous extract from Churchill's speech of 1940, 'We shall fight on the beaches, we shall fight on the landing grounds, we shall fight in the fields and on the streets, we shall fight in the hills, we shall never surrender.' Also inscribed in gold are details of the unveiling which was performed by Winston Churchill, grandson of the former Premier, on 30th November 1972. The statue was commissioned by the St. Margaret's Bay Trust.

'This plinth was presented by Marshal Tito and the people of Yugoslavia as a symbol of Yugoslavian soil, in homage to Sir Winston Churchill's leadership

48

in the war, July 23, 1969', So runs the inscription on the plaque attached to the back of the huge white rock upon which rests the seated siren-suited figure of Winston Churchill who stares at the traffic passing by. This massive bronze statue by Oscar Nemon, who was himself of Yugoslavian origin, is situated on the Green at Westerham, Kent and commemorates Sir Winston's long and cherished association with that village. Many visitors to Churchill's former home, Chartwell, some two miles south, stop to look and admire this fine monument of the reclining statesman.

In Copenhagen, Denmark, is 'Churchill Park', so named in his honour. It represents the Danish peoples' tribute to Churchill. In these pleasure grounds, since 1955, has stood on a pedestal a head and shoulders bronze portrait bust of the wartime leader to whom the Danes looked for deliverance during the occupation. This image, also by Oscar Nemon, shows Churchill wearing open neck siren suit. Nearby is the Danish Resistance Movement Museum with its many memories and souvenirs of the war years and enemy oppression.

Luxembourg, too, has a major statue of Sir Winston by Nemon. It stands in the aptly named 'Winston Churchill Place'. The cost was raised by public subscription to record the admiration and gratitude of the people of Luxembourg for the inspiring Leadership given by Churchill during the war. The figure was unveiled in 1973 and resembles the St. Margaret's Bay statue in stance, expression and movement, all symbols of an active Prime Minister. Churchill was given The Freedom of Luxembourg in 1946.

Belgium has also honoured Churchill by the erection of a statue of him. It is, again, by Nemon and is a version of the Luxembourg figure. It is situated in Winston Churchill Avenue, Brussels and was unveiled by Paul Henri Spaak, Belgian Prime Minister in October, 1967.

In Kansas City, U.S.A. is a monument which is most unusual in that it is a double statue and protrays Sir Winston and Clementine Churchill seated side by side. This late work by Nemon was cast in Hampshire and shipped to the U.S.A. for the unveiling on May 12, 1984. This task was performed by the American Ambassador to Great Britain, Charles Price. Guests at the ceremony included the sculptor, Nemon, and the Duke of Marlborough. The statue was commissioned by the English Speaking Union of the United States of America and was based on studies made by Nemon just before Churchill died in 1965. Of his work, Nemon said that there were no such monuments of the couple existing and that this one was dedicated to married love. A very unusual and fascinating inovation is a loudspeaker at the back of the statue which plays one of the Statesman's famous wartime speeches at the touch of a button. Oscar Nemon died the following year.

Halifax, Nova Scotia is the location for another statue of Sir Winston. It stands outside the Halifax City Regional Library. Again, the energetic Premier is symbolised in Oscar Nemon's figure of the striding Churchill.

Edmonton, Alberta, Canada has also a large sculpture similar to the Halifax statue.

The Principality of Monaco has a bronze portrait bust of Churchill which is situated in Winston Churchill Place. It is also by Nemon.

A number of heads and busts of Winston Churchill by Nemon are to be seen in Blenheim Palace, Chartwell, Churchill College, Cambridge, Windsor Castle, Parliament House and Conservative Party headquarters at Smith Square, London.

Churchill, so often the subject, was himself an artist of considerable talent, and tried his hand at sculpture. His model, perhaps not surprisingly, was Nemon — his tutor in this art. The result was a bronze head of Nemon which is in Churchill's studio at Chartwell.

The constituency of Woodford was represented by Winston Churchill in Parliament for some four decades. The citizens of this part of Essex, appreciative of their famous member, decided soon after his retirement from the Premiership to raise a statue of him commemorating their long and proud association. The commission was given to the sculptor David McFall and in October 1959 the stern, powerful figure, eight feet tall, was placed on its plinth at Woodford Green. This statue has a rather grim aspect but expresses the many turbulent and troubled times he endured, and the enormous weight of responsibility he bore during his long event filled years as Prime Minister and Parliamentarian. Field Marshal Montgomery unveiled the statue in the presence of Churchill himself and a very large crowd of admirers of the former leader and architect of victory in the second world war.

American people are proud that Churchill was half American by blood, and full American by the award of Honorary Citizenship. Their tremendous admiration has led to the erection of some splendid statues of him in the USA. A bronze figure by Ivor Roberts-Jones stands in British Square, New Orleans. It is eleven feet tall and, like the one in Parliament Square, is a very distinguished and masterly work. The statue was commissioned by Riverside Development Ltd and was unveiled by Lady Soames, Churchill's youngest daughter, in 1978. Winston Churchill was well remembered by many Americans on his visits to their country but on one visit in particular they recall him walking down a ship's gangway wearing naval type coat and peaked cap, friendly, jaunty, and making his famous V sign. They specified that all these fond memories of him be incorporated in the statue. Mr. Roberts-Jones was happy to comply with the request.

Outside the British Embassy in Washington is another Churchill statue, also incorporating the V sign. This massive bronze tribute, nine feet high, is by William McVey of Cleveland, and was unveiled by Randolph Churchill in 1968. Of particular interest is the fact that this figure stands with one foot on

British Territory (The Embassy Grounds) the other on American soil, symbolic of Churchill's Anglo-American parentage and his honorary citizenship of the United States of America.

To coincide with the 25th anniversary, in 1971, of the famous 'Iron Curtain' speech at Fulton, Missouri, the prominent sculptor, Franta Belsky, was commissioned to create a statue of Sir Winston to be sited at Westminster College, Fulton. The splendid, eight feet tall bronze figure of the great statesman, wearing three quarter length coat and carrying hat and walking stick, represents the fulfillment of an ambition of some thirty years which began when the young Belsky, then a soldier in the Czech Army, met Churchill. This first meeting made a very deep impression on Belsky and he started sketching, modelling and collecting material which eventually found expression in the Churchill statue. Franta Belsky's intention in this work was to portray Churchill "Standing four square in the Face of Adversity with cheerful expression of determination." It is a very competent, extremely well modelled figure. A sculptor usually makes a number of working models before the statue is finished. To attain the perfection which Mr. Belsky sought and achieved in this figure no fewer than nine models were made. The 17th century Wren Church of St Mary, Aldermanbury, London which was damaged during the blitz, was dismantled and rebuilt at Fulton where it now stands and forms part of the memorial to Churchill. The statue is close by the reconstructed church. Franta Belsky was also the sculptor of two very fine bronze busts of Churchill, one is in the foyer of the Churchill Hotel, Portman Square, London, the other is in Churchill College, Cambridge.

The Conservative Club, Hoddesdon, Hertfordshire has on display on the landing a large bronze plaque showing Churchill in relief, by Franta Belsky. Franta Belsky admired Churchill greatly and recalls that it was only the direct intervention of Churchill during the war, by sending a ship to take beleagured Czech soldiers from the collapsing France, that saved him from certain captivity by the Germans.

The Kingdom of Brunei has a very fine Museum which is unique and entirely devoted to Churchill. It forms part of the Brunei Historical and Cultural Centre opened in 1971 in the capital Kota Batu. Outside in the centre of the large crescent shaped building is a seven feet tall statue of Sir Winston Churchill. He wears the famed Cambridge hat and carries a walking stick and gloves, the right hand is raised, the fingers formed in the V salute. This is the only major statue which shows him with a cigar in the mouth. This was particularly asked for by the commissioning body. The figure portrays the buoyant, jaunty Churchill of the war years uplifting his fellow countrymen with his spirit. The statue is mounted on a very high plinth covered in black granite. The famous words of Churchill on becoming Prime Minister, "I have nothing to offer but blood, toil, tears and sweat," are inscribed in gold leaf in

English and Malay on the plinth. A picture of this statue has appeared on Brunei postage stamps. The sculptress of this very fine and impressive work was Astrid Zydower, M.B.E.

Among the many and fascinating exhibits inside the museum are three more sculptures by Astrid Zydower. These are of the greatest interest as they feature Churchill at different periods of his life and are the only known pieces as such. The first figure is the boy Winston, life size, at seven years of age, on his hands and knees playing with his cavalry soldiers. He was passionately fond of his troops. The second statue is a half size representation of the young soldier Churchill. He sits on an ammunition box at a table on which is propped a book which he reads. This item recalls his early military days when he read avidly to improve his education. The third figure is Churchill as an old man seated at the easel, under a large sun umbrella, indulging in his favourite recreation, painting. This figure is also half size and was used to illustrate Brunei postage stamps.

The Maltese 'Society of Arts, Manufacturers and Commerce' commissioned a bronze portrait bust of Sir Winston to present to him for his 80th birthday. The presentation was made at his home in Hyde Park Gate. Accompanying the bust was an illuminated address with the following text: "To the Right Honourable Sir Winston Spencer Churchill, K.G. On the initiative of the Council of the Malta Society of Arts, Manufacturers and Commerce, the People of Malta and Gozo offer you a bronze portrait bust sculpted by a Maltese Artist, as a token of their deep appreciation of your inestimable services to the British Commonwealth and Empire and to Western Civilisation. It will be a lasting pledge of their affection and gratitude for your personal interest to relieve and save Malta during her siege in the last war. To you half the world owes its freedom, democracy, its survival and justice, its triumph. In war you have led us to victory, in peace you have guided us towards security. May Divine Providence spare you in good health and happiness for many years to come, that you may yet see the fruits of your wisdom in a lasting peace among nations and a glorious revival of Christian Ideals."

It was the wish of Sir Winston that the bust be presented back to Malta in admiration of the Island's bravery during the war. The site chosen for the erection of the bust and pedestal was Upper Barrakka Gardens, Valetta overlooking the harbour, the scene of some of the fiercest activity during the war. It was unveiled by Sir Robert Laycock on 5 May, 1956. The head and shoulder sculpture was the work of Vincent Apap for whom Sir Winston sat during one of his visits to the Island. The finely detailed figure expresses the wartime leadership, courage, and determination, and the peacetime statesmanship qualities of Churchill.

In front of the house which is the headquarters of the West Essex Conservative Club in Wanstead, is a bronze head of Winston Churchill on a large white stone pedestal. It is the work of an Italian sculptor, Luigi Froni, who was interned in Britain early in the war under the Act which imprisoned alien nationals. He was an admirer of the Prime Minister and on his release during the war visited the House of Commons on a number of occasions. From the Gallery he made a series of sketches of Churchill. The bust resulted from these drawings and shows Churchill at 66 years of age. It is a comparatively early one dating from the war and may well be the first one of him made during that conflict. The Prime Minister's jaw is thrust forward and the general aspect is one of alert aggression so vital to wage and win the war. There is an interesting inscription on the nape of the neck which reads, "Nineteen forty one, The Giant of England."

Clare Sheridan completed a bronze head of Churchill in 1919. One casting from it is in the Imperial War Museum and another is owned by Mrs Raeburn Parker. This bronze from the first world war is believed to be the first sculptural representation of Churchill. On a pedestal outside the door of the Mayor's Parlour in the Town Hall, Hastings is a large bronze bust of Churchill by Clare Sheridan, who was Churchill's American cousin. It was presented to the Borough of Hastings in 1957 by Mrs. J H Downing. The original bust was sculptured in 1942 and is in Chartwell. In 1931 Churchill was seriously injured when he was knocked down by a taxi in New York. He carried a small scar on his forehead as a result of the accident, which the sculptress decided to show on the bust. Other castings of this work are at Harrow School and the Churchill Museum, Brunei.

It is unfortunate that Jacob Epstein did not produce a statue of Churchill. He did, however, sculpture a bronze head of the statesman, a casting of which is in the Imperial War Museum. It is a highly original portrait conceived in 1946, powerfully expressing the inner strength of Churchill, unflattering, almost grotesque but considered by some to be the finest of all portrait busts of the statesman. Other copies exist; one in the Queen Elizabeth the Second Conference Centre, London; another in the National Portrait Gallery, and a third in Churchill College, Cambridge. At least four others are known to exist in the United States of America.

An idea of the value of these busts can be gauged from their rare appearances at auctions. In 1966 at Christies, one realised 4800 guineas, the following year one was sold for £5,500 at Sotheby's, and in 1968 one went for 5200 guineas. The estimated value in June 1988 was £8,500. The head is in fact based on a sketch model and was not completed as Epstein intended, as Churchill, on seeing the unfinished sculpture, made known his displeasure with it. Epstein found Churchill a restless subject and felt that he had made no more than an interesting study of him. Churchill gave three sittings to Epstein at Chartwell which followed three earlier sittings at Epstein's studio.

The Prime Minister took pleasure in announcing in May 1945 that the Channel Islands which had been invaded following the fall of France and suffered five years oppressive enemy occupation, were free. The inhabitants of Jersey expressed their appreciation of Churchill's sustained leadership during the dark years by subscribing for a memorial to him. The money was raised by contributions to a 'Penny Fund' sponsored by the Jersey Evening Post. The memorial, by sculptor Anthony Gray, is a large granite stone bearing a bronze relief portrait of Sir Winston's head and shoulder, looking left. The accompanying inscription in gold leaf reads: The Right Honourable Winston Spencer Churchill, K.G.,O.M.,C.H.,. . . And our dear Channel Islands are also to be freed today 8th May 1945. The memorial was unveiled in Woodford Park, St. Brelades, on 5th December 1966 by the bailiff, Sir Robert le Masurier. The Park was renamed Sir Winston Churchill Park.

David McFall sculpted two small statues based on his large one at Woodford Green. One of the replicas is in the City Museum, Glasgow, the other is in the Church of the Holy Trinity, New York. Another example of this artist's work is in the reception hall of the Grocers' Company, Princes Street, London. The large head and shoulders bust of Sir Winston Churchill is in fact the second casting. The original was melted in the disastrous fire which almost completely destroyed the Livery hall of this ancient company. The fire which raged on 22nd September 1965 was described as the biggest in the city since the blitz.

In addition to his many major works Oscar Nemon produced a number of other bronze busts of Churchill which are privately owned. He also carved a bust of Churchill in marble which measures 22" high and is in the collection of H.M. Queen Elizabeth II; only one other is known to exist. The value is in excess of £15,000

Some bronze replicas were made of the double statue of Sir Winston and Lady Churchill in Kansas, U.S.A. The copies are 27" long and 19" high, in an edition limited to ten pieces at a cost of £5000 each. One of these is in the collection of Blenheim Palace, another in the Ashmolean Museum, Oxford. Nemon had an ambition to see a large scale version of the Kansas double statue mounted in Hyde Park but the lack of a sponsor and the proposed cost of approximately £100,000 prevented this.

A large portrait bust, 63 cm high, of Sir Winston in plaster (bronze coloured) is in the library at Bromley, Kent. It is by Elsie March, a member of a large family of painters and sculptors of international repute who lived in Bromley.

Going back to Churchill's early life, there is in the garden at the Church Street corner of the Post Office, Durban, a granite pylon bearing a bronze relief plaque of the scene when Churchill addressed a large crowd from the steps of the Town Hall on December 23rd, 1899. The inscription on the plaque reads, 'In commemoration of the speech delivered by Winston Churchill, war correspondent, from the steps of this building on December 23rd, 1899. This plaque has been erected by A. H. Smith, O.B.E., of Durban.'

Other known sculptures of Churchill are:

Head 7½" by Benjamin Clemens

Bronze Plaster Bust by Mrs. O'Donnel

Bronze bust 24" high cast in 1949 by Benno Elkan

Bust, Bronze 19" by Sir William Reid-Dick

Bust, Bronze 7" by Sir William Reid-Dick

Bust, Bronze 27.5cm by Sir William Reid-Dick

Another bust 19". One of these dates from 1942 and is in the Carlton Club, London

Bust, bronze sculptured by Leopoldo dated 1966. 38 cm.

Bust, bronze by D. Keon, 9¼" high

Bronze Head by Manassa, 13.5 cm high (144 castings)

Head, by Averill Vellacott approximately 5" high and another approximately 12" high

Bust, bronze, by Sydney Spedding.

Waist length bust of Churchill in open neck siren suit, 12" high by Albert Toft

Superb figure of Sir Winston in Garter robes, 16" high, by Karin Churchill to commemorate his 64 years as a Parliamentarian. The edition was limited to 400 but it is believed the edition is not yet complete and the figures are made to order. The cost in 1985 was 300 Pounds.

Statue of Sir Winston by Ivor Roberts-Jones 31½" tall, based on the Parliament Square figure.

Statue of Churchill in Garter Robes by Ivor Roberts-Jones 29" was displayed in Agrews British Exhibition 1975.

Bronze bust by Bryan Baker dated from 1956. 22" high.

In the National Portrait Gallery, Washington.

Soon after the war a serious but humorous proposal with plans was put forward by a Margate resident for the erection of an enormous statue of Churchill on the cliffs of Dover. The statue would in fact be a novel form of Lighthouse with the cigar lit up and revolving as the warning light was flashed to ships in the Channel.

A SURVEY OF PORTRAITURE OF SIR WINSTON CHURCHILL

Randolph Churchill once remarked of his father 'that he was the most photographed of men'. The same statement may be applied regarding paintings of Churchill for he was surely the most artistically portrayed of men. Many artists attracted by the magnetism of Churchill sought to capture some aspect of him and set down in oils, or other mediums, their impression. A number of fortunate artists were privileged to be granted sittings and their efforts, in widely differing styles, provide an enrichment to the world of art.

Besides the formal statesman type of portrait which one would expect, there is a fine selection of uniformed pictures, as befits a man who liked dressing up, and which remind us of his strong connections with the Army, Navy and Air Force. There are also splendid portraits of Churchill in ceremonial uniforms and Robes, signifying his love of tradition and pride in the various appointments he held. Some of these had their origins deep in history and were rather quaint. Sir Winston was also fondly pictured by artists in his siren suit which he took to wearing during the war.

Churchill himself was an artist, and it was natural that he numbered among his friends several painters of renown; Sickert, Nicholson, Lavery and Orpen. When he sat for an artist he always took a keen interest in what was going on. Bernard Hailstone relates how, when he was painting Churchill, he found it quite disconcerting when, from time to time, Churchill would rise from his chair, walk over to him, and peer over his shoulder to see how he was progressing.

What is possibly the first portrait of Churchill was painted in 1901 by Edwin A. Ward to be used as an illustration in a book called Recollections of a Savage! It pictures an earnest young Churchill seated at his desk writing, facing the artist. It is unlikely that this was from life, but was probably based on one of the early photographs such as those which were used on cigarette cards issued at the time. Ward painted Churchill's father and the same chair is used by the sitters in both portraits.

The first period of major portraiture of Churchill dates from the first world war when he was in his very early forties. Some very important studies by five artists were completed during the first years of the conflict.

On the wall facing the stairs at the National Liberal Club, Whitehall Place, London, hangs a full length, life size, dramatic portrait of Churchill in dashing military dress uniform with medals and sword, he was First Lord of the Admiralty when it was painted. It is by Ernest Townsend, an American, and was presented anonymously to the club in 1915. Originally the portrait hung in the club's smoking room but was taken down as a mark of displeasure soon after Churchill crossed the House of Commons in 1924 and re-joined the Conservatives. It was restored to favour after the end of the second world war, although it is not displayed with other Liberal Prime Ministers' portraits. The picture was damaged by enemy action in an air raid during the war and repaired in 1947.

Winston Churchill was First Lord when he was painted by Sir William Guthrie. This was a half length portrayal of him wearing formal dark dress and shows Churchill with his right elbow resting on a table with the right hand supporting his head. This powerful study is in the National Portrait Gallery of Scotland, in Edinburgh.

About 1915, after his resignation from the Admiralty, Churchill sat for Sir William Orpen. The resulting portrait was presented to him by Lord Rothermere. Churchill, dressed in black, stands with his left hand on hip, holding his hat in the other hand. It has been suggested that the strain of the Dardenelles failure, the blame that he bore, and his subsequent departure from the Admiralty, are reflected in the solemn expression. This masterly three quarter length painting was copied in 1962 by John Leigh-Pemberton. The copy is in the dining room of Churchill College, Cambridge; the original is owned by a member of the Churchill family.

Another fine but contrasting half length portrait from the same period depicts Churchill, with pensive face, in army uniform, wearing the blue French steel helmet which he favoured. The picture was painted by his friend, Sir John Lavery, R.A., and is a very compelling reminder of Churchill's active military service during the first world war when he shared with his men the discomforts and extreme dangers of trench warfare. The painting was given to him by the officers of the Armoured Car Squadrons for his devoted efforts on their behalf. It hangs at Chartwell on the wall opposite the stairs with the steel helmet hanging below. This portrait was pointed out to Bernard Hailstone by Sir Winston with the remark, "That is when they thought I was a gonner."

Sir John Lavery also painted Churchill during his term as First Lord of the Admiralty. It is a half length portrait of Churchill with his body turned to the left, and he sits with arms folded across his chest looking at the artist. This picture is in the Municipal Gallery of Modern Art, Dublin. Another painting by this artist shows Churchill standing, facing his easel with brushes and paints, working on a picture. The title of this work is "The Blue Bay. Mr. Churchill on the Riviera, 1921."

In 1916 an impression of Churchill was completed by Ambrose McEvoy, which was for a time in Toronto, Ontario, Canada. The painting, of a serious, formally dressed Churchill was exhibited at the Leicester Gallery, London in 1953. Later it was purchased by an unnamed Parliamentary person.

The front page cover of the Illustrated London News, 25 April 1925, featured a full page photo etching of Winston Churchill when he was Chancellor of the Exchequer. This superb illustration was by James Bacon & Sons and bore the caption, 'The Minister to whom the taxpayer looks for relief under the forthcoming budget.' The unusual technique employed made this an outstanding portrait.

Another portrayal of the Chancellor in 1925 was by John Singer Sargent which is charcoal on paper. This picture is now in Chartwell, Churchill's former home.

A study by Walter Sickert of Churchill was completed in 1927. This artist was a friend who sometimes stayed at Chartwell, he also gave tuition in various techniques of painting to Churchill. The Sickert portrait is a head and shoulder study of Churchill in thoughtful mood holding a lighted cigar. A somewhat blotchy and indistinct impression of the Chancellor of the Exchequer, this portrait hangs in the National Portrait Gallery.

An interesting back view of Churchill, seated, painting and entitled, 'Painting under the Loggia at Chartwell,' was by Churchill himself. The picture was exhibited at the Knoedler Gallery, London in 1977. It was available for purchase then at 20,000 Pounds.

About 1929, Churchill painted another self portrait in which he depicts himself in an apron, standing by his easel with a palette in one hand and a brush in the other. The back of this picture is inscribed, 'Self portrait painted by my husband.'

An epic painting by Sir James Guthrie portrays an assembled group of 17 prominent British Politicians of the first world War. The scene is entirely imaginary and does not record or commemorate any actual occasion. Qualification for inclusion was that the statesman had held office at the outbreak of war up to the time of the armistice (Kitchener was drowned when H.M.S.'Hampshire' was sunk in 1916 but was posthumously included).

The distinguished personalities, five of whom attained the Office of Prime Minister, are sitting or standing round a conference table discussing matters of great importance and urgency. Significantly, perhaps, Churchill occupies a central position with eight colleagues on either side of him. Extra emphasis is added by an oblique ray of sunlight which shines down from the right like a spotlight illuminating the tenacious Churchill, who gazes with the countenance of a visionary into the future. Some have speculated that the ray was a prophetic sign of his future greatness. Sir James Guthrie studied group portraits by Frans Hals, and his treatment of the assembled statesmen reveals this influence by the 17th century Dutch painter. For dramatic effect the meeting is taking place in a theatrical setting, which could be anywhere, with an oriental screen behind and to the right of the debaters. The background is dominated by the huge headless statue of Nike the Winged Victory of

Samothrace from the Louvre, flanked by enormous Doric columns.

The Statesmen who appear with Churchill are: The Maharaja of Bikaner, Louis Botha, George Nicol Barnes, Sir Robert Laird Border, Arthur James Balfour, Sir Eric Campbell Geddes, Andrew Bonar Law, Baron Morris, Lord Kitchener, Sir Joseph Cook, Wm. Morris Hughes, David Lloyd George, Viscount Milner, William Fergusson Massey, Edward Grey, Herbert Asquith.

The masterpiece is entitled, 'Some Statesmen of the Great War' and was one of a series of three paintings commissioned by Sir A. Bailey for the National Portrait Gallery. The other two pictures were "Some Generals and Officers of the Great War" and 'Some Naval Officers of the Great War.' Sir James Guthrie spent six years working on this enormous picture which measures 13' x 11'. It was completed in 1930, just a few months before the death of the artist. Six of the portrayed statesmen died before it was finished.

Sir William Nicholson painted Winston Churchill and Clementine Churchill seated at a table at Chartwell. The picture dates from 1934-1936 and is entitled, 'The Churchills at breakfast.'

The second world war represents another period when some major inspired and accomplished portraits of the Prime Minister were completed. One of the first paintings to appear from that period was by Professor Arthur Pan, an eminent artist of Hungarian origin who came to Britain shortly before the war began. His picture is dated 1942 and is a formal impression of Churchill seated on a leather backed chair holding a cigar in his right hand. It is an extremely fine study of the Premier, at the height of his power, with a characteristically serious expression. The picture was first published by Frost and Reed in 1943 and was issued with the intention that proceeds from the sale of the first 1000 copies were donated to Mrs Churchill's 'Aid to Russia' fund. Professor Pan's portrait of the Prime Minister hangs in the Great Hall of the Merchant Venturers.

This artist made an earlier study of Churchill in 1941. This is a half length portrait and shows the Prime Minister seated, looking left. He wears a dark suit with waistcoat and bow tie. The expression is thoughtful.

A number of portraits of the Premier were painted by Frank Salisbury. One of these hangs in the library at Chartwell. It portrays Churchill wearing blue siren suit, seated at his desk, holding in his right hand a pen and spectacles. He is pictured as he looks up during a pause in his work. This study was completed in 1942. An almost identical version of this picture was presented to Harrow School in 1943. There is, however, more detail in this one, for instance a cigar and an envelope with wax seal are included. In the top right hand corner is a small motif of a mounted knight in armour under the banner of St. George. A formal portrait by this artist appeared in the journal 'Womans Own' March, 1943. Salisbury also painted a standing half length study of the Premier in dark suit and bow tie. Several further portraits by Salisbury have identical poses by Churchill, he stands with his left hand on the hip, while the other hand hangs down and holds a book which is on the table. In one of the pictures he is formally attired — this portrait is in the Constitutional Club. A similar painting hangs in Number 10 Downing Street. Another painting presents him dressed in the impressive gold and black robes of Chancellor of Bristol University, where the portrait hangs. A seated impression of Churchill, in sombre suit appeared in 'The Horse' magazine, part 26, 1975. The original of this picture is in the collection of the Jockey Club at Newmarket.

A major painting by Frank Salisbury is of the scene at the Guildhall when Churchill received the Freedom of the City of London on 30 June, 1943. This splendid picture was found to contain several inaccuracies when completed which the Library Committee insisted must be rectified. The form which this ancient ceremony took was that the casket, made from damaged roof timber from Guildhall, containing the Certificate of Freedom, remained on the table while the Chamberlain, Sir Adrian Pollock, extended the right hand of Friendship to Churchill. The artist, however, originally showed the Chamberlain presenting Churchill with the casket. Other mistakes were that the Lord Chancellor and the Archbishop of Canterbury were portrayed in their ceremonial robes which they had not worn for the occasion, and also that the principal personages were shown in rearranged positions. This was because Salisbury considered that for the picture to have a correct balance of colour it was necessary to show the Archbishop and Lord Chancellor in their robes, and also the rearrangement of the figures would give a more dramatic composition. Salisbury believed that the casket was the focal point of the picture and was reluctant to alter anything. However, the Library Committee thought that the painting should be a faithful and accurate record of an important city event. A compromise was reached and it was agreed that the position of the casket be altered to its present place on the table while the Chamberlain extends his hand in friendship. Salisbury believed that his painting was marred by the correction and that the casket now looked like nothing more than Churchill's cigar box. Distinguished personalities in the picture include Mrs Churchill, Mary Churchill, Mrs. Duncan Sandys, Mrs. Vic Oliver, Anthony Eden, Clement Attlee and the Duke of Marlborough. The painting was the gift to the Corporation of the City of London from Sir Samuel Joseph who, as Lord Mayor, had presided over the ceremony. It was presented privately on his behalf by his wife and son on 30 November, 1944, Churchill's 70th birthday. The picture measures 58" x 110".

Churchill is dramatically portrayed in a painting by F G Kwarta. He is clad in an overcoat, buttoned up to the neck, and stands by the beach with the white cliffs of Dover in the background. He holds a walking stick horizontally in the right hand. The dark, heavy clouds behind him symbolise the great peril threatening Britain, and the loneliness of his high office during wartime is conveyed by the mood of solitude evoked by this picture. The painting may be seen in the studio at Chartwell.

A number of artists have elected to portray Churchill with a background of book-lined shelves. Such a setting was chosen by Robert Russell in his painting of the Premier in a siren suit and holding a cigar. Russell also painted a picture of the Prime Minister, in evening dress and top hat, and holding up his right hand in acknowledgement. This was copied from a photograph which appeared in a newspaper dated 1941.

Following the armistice between France and Germany of 1940, Churchill was extremely concerned over the dangerous possibility that the powerful French fleet of warships, anchored at Oran, Algeria, would be seized by the Germans and added to their fleet to be eventually used against the Allies. To forestall this likelihood a British Naval force arrived at Oran on 3rd July, 1940. Terms were offered to the French Commander giving him a choice of three alternative ways to save his ships from being captured by the Axis forces. He was informed with regret that unless he accepted the terms his fleet would be destroyed within six hours. He refused the terms and a short engagement ensued during which one French battleship was sunk and the other ships badly damaged.

The next day Churchill spoke to the House of Commons relating the sombre details. It had been a traumatic experience for him, but, after listening attentively and silently to his speech the House erupted with everybody standing and cheering. The action of destroying the French fleet had signalled that Britain, far from being vulnerable or indecisive had the capacity to strike ruthlessly.

The Illustrated London News commissioned the artist Terence Cuneo to capture for its readers the scene at the House of Commons when Churchill had just finished making the Oran speech. Cuneo's dramatic portrayal shows the Prime Minister sitting with his head held in his hands and the M.Ps on their feet cheering in acclamation at his speech. The former Prime Minister, Neville Chamberlain and the deputy Premier, Clement Attlee, are seen applauding Churchill. This picture appeared in the Illustrated London News dated 13 July, 1940.

A seated portrait of Churchill with an intense but friendly expression was painted in 1944 by W. Bouvard. The Prime Minister is facing right and has his hand in his jacket pocket with the thumb jutting out.

Several paintings of the wartime Churchill were completed by Alfred Eggerton Cooper. One of these was used as a front cover illustration for 'Tatler' Magazine, 5th May, 1943. It was of the dark suited Premier facing left, with a sheaf of documents on his knee, and holding a cigar from which smoke is coiling. The title of this picture was 'Profile for Victory.' A similar portrait is in the Carlton Club. Cooper next painted two portraits with identical poses, one shows the Prime Minister seated, in black coat and striped trousers, in his library with rows of book-lined shelves in the background. The other is of Churchill sitting on a bench in a garden with a large tree immediately behind him. This artist also did a pastel study of Churchill soon after the end of the war in which he is attired in evening dress and wearing the cross and insignia of the Order of Merit which he was awarded in 1946. This impression was sold for sixty guineas at an auction in 1974. A later painting by Cooper of Churchill, again in evening dress but additionally he wears the Sash of the Order of the Garter, dates from the mid 1950's. The same seated pose as in the garden picture is used.

With the end of the war came rcognition that Churchill was one of history's greatest men, and it was not surprising that many artists sought to portray him. The choice of dress in which to present him had become even wider with the addition of the uniform of Lord Warden of the Cinque Ports. An exceptionally attractive painting of 1946 by Douglas Chandor portrays Churchill in Royal Air Force uniform with the rank of honorary Air Commodore, wearing pilot's wings and many medal ribbons. He is hatless, seated and holding spectacles in his left hand. On the table to his left is an open box of matches and an ashtray holding a lighted cigar. This picture appeared in a publication interestingly entitled 'Fifty American Faces' and also 'Woman's Journal' December, 1957. It is in the collection of the National Portrait Gallery, Washington. It was painted at the request of President Truman.

One of the first artists to paint Churchill from life after the war was Arthur Hayward. His three quarter length standing portrait shows the then, Leader of the Opposition in a grey suit holding a cigar. This very accomplished work is in the University of Kent, Canterbury.

John Spencer Churchill, a nephew, completed several paintings of Sir Winston. One portrait was inscribed in the top right hand corner, 'to Winston on his 80th birthday.' Two pictures from this artist show Sir Winston wearing his siren suit, painting on his easel at Chartwell. Another shows Churchill in open neck siren suit, peering over his spectacles. This impression was sold for 75 Pounds in 1971.

A very good likeness of Churchill was achieved by Stella Schmelle in her half length portrait of him in evening dress, wearing the cross and insignia of the Order of Merit. This picture realised 450 Pounds when sold in 1977.

Some examples of Graham Sutherland's work concerning Churchill may be seen in the National Portrait Gallery. There are some sketches made in 1954 and a painting of an aging rather grim Churchill. The Gallery also has in its possession a number of notes and drawings by Sutherland which he made in preparation for his portraits. These include sketches of Churchill's hands and facial features; there is even a drawing of Churchill asleep. A study for an impression of Churchill by this artist was exhibited in April 1975 at the Le

Feure Gallery, London.

Churchill sat for Sutherland in 1954, when several portraits were completed, one of these is a fine full length impression of Sir Winston wearing Garter Robes. This picture is in the Beaverbrook Art Gallery, Fredericton, N.B., Canada. One of the studies which resulted from the sittings was the controversial portrait, which was the gift of the House of Commons to Churchill for his 80th birthday. When it was presented to him in Westminster Hall, he described it as 'a remarkable example of modern art.' The painting was quite unflattering and of severe aspect. Churchill took a dislike to it; he thought it made him look a halfwit. His hands were small and soft, and he did not like the way that the artist had shown them as somewhat large and coarse. The feet were not included in the painting. After spending some eleven months hidden from sight at Chartwell, the painting was destroyed on the instructions of Lady Churchill. This was a great tragedy and a severe loss to the world of art.

The destroyed portrait has a fascination for many people, particularly artists, and it was inevitable that some would attempt to imitate it. A copy was made, from photographs, by Donald Clarke. It was a reasonable likeness but with the harshness taken out and it portrayed a far more benign Churchill than the original. This imitation realised 200 Pounds when sold in an auction. Another attempt to reproduce it was an altogether different affair. It was in fact a superb effort by the German artist Albrecht von Leyden. His reconstruction was to serve as a protest to the destruction of the original portrait. He spent two years researching the work and many months more, painting, but he achieved a highly creditable result. Finally, as a touch of humour he painted on the back of the canvas, "We shall never surrender."

A portrait also dating from the mid 1950's was painted by Max Nauta, who was one of Holland's foremost artists in glass and portraiture. He was given four sittings at Chartwell by Churchill in 1955 or just before. To Nauta, Churchill appeared as a formidable square figure, full of life and activity. The liberal use of vibrant reds and greens in the picture are expressive of this vitality. Churchill said to Nauta that a good portrait is a rare thing. Sir Winston was very pleased with the painting and said, 'It is admirable, excellent.' In the picture Churchill is seated by a table on which are some books, a few standing and some lying, and also two or three papers. His right hand, which holds his spectacles, is resting on an open book. The left arm hangs down over the chair armrest and the hand holds a cigar. This very fine impression of Sir Winston hangs in the reception hall of the Lower House of the Dutch Parliament, to whom it was presented on completion by a Dutchman who lived in England.

A sensitive study by Sir Oswald Birley depicts Churchill seated by a table which is covered by a green cloth on which rests his right arm. He is formally dressed in black jacket and pin striped trousers. The portrait is dated 1946, when Churchill was Leader of the Opposition, and was presented to the house of Commons by Sir Robert Rankin, M.P. Sir Oswald Birley completed several other fine paintings of Sir Winston, but these were dated 1951. One portrait of him in open neck siren suit was acquired by the National Trust for display at Chartwell. A very similar painting is owned by Lady Soames.

Among the many and varied offices held by Churchill, one which gave him pleasure and appealed to his sense of the romantic, was that of Elder Brother of the Corporation of Trinity House. This ancient fraternity has its roots deep in history and was already a guild of mariners of some importance when granted its first Royal Charter by Henry VIII in 1514. The present day responsibility of the corporation is the administration of lighthouses, light vessels, and the control of pilotage, buoys, and beacons around the coasts of Britain, the Channel Islands and Gibraltar. Churchill was First Lord of the Admiralty when he was appointed honorary Elder Brother of Trinity House in 1913. He was very fond of wearing, on suitable occasions, the attractive and impressive uniform that went with the appointment. Sir Winston is shown in the uniform of a Captain of Trinity House in a portrait by Oswald Birley in 1951. He is seated on a chair with his left arm on the armrest and the right hand on his knee. His hat is on a table to the right.

Another ancient office held with pride by Sir Winston was Lord Warden of the Cinque Ports. The origin of this office may be traced back to Roman times when a special system of defence for the south east coast of England was devised against invaders from Scandinavia and the Baltic. Later, the Saxons adapted the system which was based on five ports which were known as the Cinque Ports — Hastings, Hythe, New Romney, Dover and Sandwich. The towns of Rye and Winchelsea were eventually added. Churchill was appointed Lord Warden and Admiral of the Cinque Ports and Constable of Dover Castle in 1941 and installed in August 1946 by the Grand Council of Shepway. The portrait, by Oswald Birley, of Churchill in Trinity House dress was being copied in 1953 by John Leigh-Pemberton when he decided to change the uniform to that of Lord Warden. He then added the Sash and Decoration of the Order of the Garter. John Leigh-Pemberton was the only artist whom Lady Birley would allow to copy the portraits. This copy is in the National Maritime Museum, Greenwich, the original hangs in Trinity House.

In 1945 or 1946 Charles Ernest Wallcousins portrayed Churchill in a book-lined room standing behind a desk on which is resting a map of the world. The setting is likely to be the office of Leader of the Opposition at the House of Commons. The artist has used various appropriate symbols as a decorative backcloth; the motif of St. George and the Dragon appears together with the emblems of England and Scotland — the Rose and the Thistle — whilst a winged trident on a defensive shield is also present. the portrait was used as the frontispiece of 'The Victory Book' published by Odhams Press in 1946.

Bernard Hailstone R.P., was privileged to paint the last major studies from life of Winston Churchill, his impressions thus have an added interest which must enhance their value in future years. Winston Churchill sat for Hailstone at Chartwell and No. 10 Downing Street in 1955, this was the year following the Sutherland sittings. He confided to Hailstone that he thought the Sutherland portrait made him look like a half dead thing. What is of considerable interest is the fact that Churchill was working on 'The History of the English Speaking Peoples' at that time and utilised some of his posing hours to dictate passages of this massive work.

Hailstone completed a varied selection of portraits from the sittings. One is of Churchill majestically dressed in the uniform of Lord Warden of the Cinque Ports; a full length, life size picture which now hangs appropriately in Dover Town Hall. He also did a waist length version of this portrait which he retained. He then painted two portraits of Churchill, in a light coloured suit, looking to the left. One of these, a small head and shoulder study of wistful expression, is in the National Portrait Gallery. The other, which pleased Churchill, is a waist length painting of Sir Winston holding a cigar. It measures 36" x 28" and was sold to a private collector in America. Hailstone also painted a small picture of a khaki clad Churchill which was sent to a gallery in Canada. Finally, there is a half length portrait of Sir Winston in open neck siren suit.

A charming study by Rhoda Birley, painted in 1956, shows Churchill with Lady Clementine seated at a table. Sir Winston is wearing a stetson type hat and is amusing himself with playing cards. The picture is entitled, 'In the Loggia' and measures 25" x 30".

In the 'Atlantic Advocate,' July 1946, appeared a painting of Churchill, by David Jagger, in which he is wearing a striped suit and holding a cigar. The pose is rather unusual as it shows Churchill with the right leg crossed over the left leg. A caption beneath the picture proclaims, 'His name became another term for good temper, good wit, good feeling for his fellow men.'

A very detailed painting by A.R. Thomson, R.A. depicts the scene in the House of Commons. The title of this impressive and interesting picture is, 'The Debate on the Address in the House of Commons.' Hundreds of M.Ps are present, many of whom are quite easily recognised, including Sir Winston Churchill, who is clearly seen sitting on the front bench. The Prime Minister, Harold MacMillan, is on his feet making a speech and the Leader of the Opposition, Hugh Gaitskill, listens attentively. Other prominent politicians included are Jo Grimmond, George Brown, Ian MacLeod, R.A. Butler, Edward Heath, Gerald Nabarro, James Callaghan and Harold Wilson. The picture was exhibited at the Royal Academy in 1963, the size is 59" x 71".

A.R. Thomson also painted a half length portrait of Churchill gripping his left lapel and holding a cigar in the right hand.

Winston Churchill was portrayed in his Garter Robes by Edward Halliday in 1957. He also made a very fine sketch showing Sir Winston seated and wearing a siren suit. This drawing was sold for 65 Pounds.

Thomas C. Dugdale R.A. completed a half length portrait showing Churchill gripping his right lapel. This painting realised 60 Pounds when sold in 1969.

The prominent artist John Leigh-Pemberton was commissioned by the brewers, Whitbreads, to paint copies of three well known photographs of Churchill. These were:

1. The siege of Sydney Street where Churchill as Home Secretary visited the scene.

2. The picture from the second world war when he is seen surveying the bomb damage at the House of Commons.

3. Sir Winston sitting by a waterway, on which are boats and ducks, painting.

The size of all three attractive and accomplished paintings is approximately 24" x 20". They date from 1951.

An outstanding painting of recent years is by George A Campbell in which Churchill is portrayed in the uniform of a colonel, tie removed, relaxing while visiting 3rd Division at Schloss Moyland during the crossing of the Rhine. He has a cigar in his mouth and holds a box of matches in the left hand. In the picture he is wearing the cap and collar badges of the Royal Sussex Regiment as Lord Warden of the Cinque Ports. This painting is based on a photograph which shows Churchill sitting on an armoured car.

A water colour by Francis Russell Flint depicts an active scene shortly after the Normandy landings. Churchill, in naval type dress and peaked cap, is wearing a life jacket and is on board a vessel crossing the Channel. He is accompanied by a number of allied military and naval leaders. The title of this stirring war scene is 'On the Bridge, H.M.S. Kelvin, D. Day plus 9'. This painting realised 400 Pounds when sold in an auction in May 1980.

In the Town Hall, Deal, Kent, hangs a superb three quarter length portrait of Sir Winston, resplendent in the Uniform of Lord Warden of the Cinque Ports, against the white cliffs of Dover. The painting is by Dennis Ramsay and the cost was raised by public subscription. An inscription below the portrait records that Sir Winston was an honorary Freeman of Deal from 1951 until 1965.

High on the wall in the studio at Chartwell hangs a painting by an unknown Russian artist of the three wartime leaders, Stalin, Roosevelt and Churchill, conferring together during the meeting which took place at Yalta in the Crimea, February 1945. Stalin was the only leader to remain in power six months after the meeting as Roosevelt died in April and Churchill was deposed in July.

Many photographs were taken of Churchill and Roosevelt during the Atlantic Conference on board H.M.S. "Prince of Wales", August 1941. One of the photographs was reproduced as an oil painting by Raymond Wilson, the picture shows the two leaders seated side by side engaged in conversation. The painting was the property of Lady Churchill who presented it after some years to Trinity House Corporation, London where it now hangs.

Other known paintings of Churchill are by:

Julian Lamar, which hangs in the University of Texas.
C.C. Michelson, which is in the Dallas Museum of Friendship.
Roger Mory, an oil on board portrait, in Crewkern, Somerset.
Robert Tollash. A portrait of Sir Winston wearing light colour suit, and with a saintly appearance, sold for £220 in 1965.
Grace Wheatley, a pictorial fantasy with many scenes from his life, from Victoria to Elizabeth, entitled "The Statesman."
George de Piro, Churchill seated before a balcony.
Cecil A. Fabian.
Jessie Hayden.
Gloria Smith, entitled, 'Songs at Harrow.'
Marjorie Forbes, two portraits.
Ruskin-Spear R.A. Churchill broadcasting before a microphone.
This picture was exhibited at the Royal Academy, Summer 1957.
Thomas Edgar Stephens. Churchill in dark striped suit, a very bold study.
Eugenia M. Shelley. An American artist who painted a head and shoulder study with a background of book-filled shelves.
B. Rawlings. An earnest 12" x 10" portrait, with a scroll below giving dates of birth and death of Churchill.
Tom Cox. Excellent portrait of Churchill with left hand on hip and right hand pressing down on walking stick.
Rhoda Birley. Picture of Churchill in an orange grove.
Ernest Hamlin Baker. Portrait in water colour. In the collection of the National Portrait Gallery, Washington.
Paul Dyeth — A study of Churchill in Garter Robes.

An unusual art form which features Churchill is the Hastings Embroidery. It was commissioned to commemorate the 900th anniversary of the Battle of Hastings and may be seen in the Town Hall there.

It presents a pageant of British History colourfully and skilfully portrayed in 27 panels. Eighty one great events and occasions are symbolically pictured beginning with the Battle of Hastings and including Magna Carta, Raleigh, Drake, Nelson, Trafalgar, The Boston Tea Party, Boer War and the two great world wars.

Sir Winston Churchill rightly has his place in this fine pictorial record. He appears in the final panel and was chosen to symbolise the spirit of Great Britain and her history. An unusual back view of him is shown. He stands facing the sea looking at British aircraft in wartime camouflage flying out on a mission. His right arm is raised in the V salute to them. The winkle shell pictured is a reminder of the gold winkle presented to him to denote his membership of this charitable organisation. The accompanying panel shows that part of S.E. England which includes the Cinque Ports. Churchill held the ancient Office of Lord Warden of the Cinque Ports from 1941 until his death in 1965. This magnificent embroidery was made by the Royal School of Needlework, it is 74 metres long and took 22 needlewomen 10 months to complete.

There is another example of needlework by the same school, which is known as the Overlord Embroidery. This fine work of applique might well be termed the modern counterpart of the Bayeux Tapestry. It captures in vivid needleworked detail the tension filled days in wartime Britain following the Dunkirk evacuation. Dramatically portrayed are scenes of the Battle of Britain, The Blitz and the Battle of the Atlantic. The embroidery pictures the gradual turning of the tide, the growing strength of the Allies, the meticulous planning by the commanders of the coming invasion of Europe. It graphically shows the mighty air and sea armadas, bearing large armies of soldiers, crossing the channel, and then the hard fought battles.

Just a few days after the landings H.M. King George VI and Churchill toured the Normandy beaches. A scene in the Embroidery shows the King and Prime Minister with Generals Eisenhower and Montgomery and Field Marshall Brook on board ship, with the prefabricated Mulberry Harbour in the background.

The work was commissioned by Lord Dulverton and took five years to make, being completed in 1973. It measures over 80 metres in length and is one metre deep. Twenty needlewomen were employed on the 34 panels. The designer was Sandra Lawrence. For a few years the embroidery was on view at Chiswell House, the headquarters of Whitbread's Brewery. It was given to the nation by Lord Dulverton. It is now on view in the Portsmouth D. Day Museum.

On the floor of the north vestibule at the National Gallery, Churchill is illustrated and takes pride of place at the centre of a series of 15 mosaic pictures. The series is called, 'The Modern Virtues' and was laid during Autumn 1952 and opened on 25 November same year.

The Churchill mosaic is entitled 'Defiance' and he is seen standing before the white cliffs of Dover, dressed in the famous siren suit, wearing a steel helmet and making the V sign. He defies a crowned apocalyptic beast in the shape of a swastika who rules a defeated Europe and now threatens Britain. This very fine and rare form of art work is made entirely of marble. It is the work of Boris Anrep, 1885-1969. The other virtues in the series are:

Compassion, Compromise, Curiosity, Delectation, Folly, Humour, Leisure, Lucidity, Open Mind, Pursuit, Sixth Sense, Wonder, Here I Lie, and Rest and be Thankful.

A place where one would undoubtedly expect to find an image of Sir Winston Churchill is Madame Tussauds in Marylebone Road, London. This most famous surviving exhibition of wax portraits was founded in Paris in 1770, moved to England in 1802, and settled in London in 1835. Tussauds is a great tourist attraction with an unrivalled display of lifelike figures of famous and infamous, national and international, past and present celebrities from all walks of life. The exhibition attracts two million visitors every year.

The first waxwork portrait of Churchill was exhibited in 1909 soon after his marriage. He has been represented at Tussauds ever since and the present effigy of him, which is believed to be the thirteenth, was made in 1978. Some current figures have their spell of glory in Tussauds but with diminishing fame they are eventually taken out of the display. In the case of outstanding personalities however their effigies are permanently on show. Naturally while the wax portrait represents a living person a new model is called for from time to time to show the corresponding aging of the famous subject. Usually the celebrity gives sittings for the sculptors; Churchill sat for Tussauds artists on several occasions between 1939 and 1952. The sculptor of at least three versions of Churchill wax portraits was Bernard Tussaud, the last of the famous family to be actively involved there.

The current figure of Sir Winston Churchill, a splendid image, stands in the great hall in a group of former Prime Ministers; Lloyd-George, Harold MacMillan and Benjamin Disraeli. The wax portraits take approximately 3-4 months to achieve the lifelike appearance.

There is also a branch of Madame Tussauds in Amsterdam and the current model of Churchill there was made in London.

In Copenhagen, there is a wax exhibition known as Louis Tussaud which has on display a figure of Churchill. The Danish Tussauds has no connection with Madame Tussauds, London.

No town or village High Street would be complete without its public house or inn, identified and made prominent by a colourful, distinctive sign. Pub signs can be traced back hundreds of years, they are often steeped in history and are supposed to have originated largely because of the illiteracy of the population and the resultant need for them to be able to identify various premises. The familiar signs are now established as part of Britain's tradition.

Some of them are painted by artists of considerable talent and might well qualify as works of art in their own right. The range of subjects on signs is endless with past members of Royal Families and the aristocracy, and famous persons being particularly popular. To have a public house named after a person represents a lasting tribute to him.

A number of public house owners, inspired by the life of Churchill, have named their premises after him. There are approximately a score of pubs dedicated to his memory, most of which are located in the southern part of England. An interesting and varied selection of outdoor portraits of Sir Winston is thus displayed in this open air gallery, worthy of inclusion in this book. Most of the pubs were formerly known by other names but since Churchill's heroic war years they have been retitled to carry his name.

The Churchill Inn, Paxford, Chipping Camden. This Inn was established in 1956 having been developed from an off licence. The village and surrounding area have many connections with another branch of the Churchill family. The picture on the sign shows Churchill wearing a dark suit, bow tie, hat and with a cigar in his mouth. He is making the famous V sign with the raised right hand. A large unfurled Union Jack dominates the top left hand corner.

The Churchill, West Lavington, near Devizes. Lying on the road to Salisbury and quite popular with travellers, this establishment is also a restaurant and conference centre. The sign features a striking head and shoulders portrait of Sir Winston with strong, well defined features, wearing a brown suit and bow tie. The artist is Stanley Chew who is well known for his attractive signs.

Winston Churchill Restaurant and Pub. This inn nestles at the foot of Ide Hill which is between Sevenoaks and Edenbridge, Kent. It is an ideal place to have a meal and refreshment after having visited Chartwell which is some five miles distant. It is very comfortable and provides excellent food. On the walls are displayed some very interesting pictures, cartoons and photographs of Churchill. There are also paintings by a local artist of Sir Winston's racehorses, one of whom was the famous 'Columnist'. The sign portrays a waist length painting of Churchill wearing a sombre suit with bow tie.

Sir Winston Churchill Public House. A fine pub which is on the Raleigh Road in the village of Hutton some two miles from Shenfield. It was formerly very run down and called 'The Plough' but the new owner, an admirer of Churchill, decided after extensive alterations and rebuilding to rename it after the great statesman. The sign was painted by a local artist and portrays a younger Churchill with rather more hair than he actually had and looking somewhat like a film star. An extra long cigar, from which smoke rises vertically, is in the right corner of his mouth. This pub has a few items of Churchill memorabilia inside and the owner is in the process of building up an interesting collection.

The Winston Churchill, Dunstable. This public house is a fairly new building situated in the High Street of this Bedfordshire town some 35 miles north of London. Meals are available in the restaurant or at the bar. The present sign is a very imaginative impression, rather than a portrait, of Churchill wearing naval type jacket with yachting cap. A cigar is in his mouth and a red lanyard, supporting an unseen pair of binoculars, hangs from his neck. With the right hand he makes the usual V sign. The portrait is set against a background of the sea with a warship in the top right hand corner. This sign replaced one showing a more conventional portrait of Sir Winston and caused considerable controversy in the town over the unflattering portrayal of Churchill. The extensive correspondence in the local press led to the matter being reported in the national newspapers and on television.

The Winston Churchill Public House, Debden. Situated just a few miles from Woodford, Churchill's former constituency, this pub occupies a modern building on a corner position. It has two different, but very good portraits, one on either side of the sign board. One picture is of a nonchalant Churchill dressed in double breasted blue jacket and yachting cap, cigar in mouth, binoculars slung round neck and making the V sign. The other picture shows a very good likeness of a formally attired Churchill with his left hand in the trouser pocket and the other hand raised in the familiar V salute.

The Churchill Arms, Kensington Church Street, London. This pub, near Notting Hill, was once known as 'Church-on-the-Hill' but was renamed some years ago. Inside is a very good selection of photographs, sketches and memorabilia relating to Sir Winston. It is a traditional type pub with bar meals available. The sign is superb and must be one of the best with a very fine portrayal of Churchill wearing his Garter Robes.

The Churchill, at Churchill, Somerset. This village used to be the seat of the Churchill family and is where the ancestors of the Dukes of Marlborough came from. The sign features Sir Winston in dark suit with Cambridge hat, cigar in mouth and his right hand raised with the V sign. In the background flames and smoke recall the war years and the blitz.

Churchills, Silvertown. This part of Woolwich is the setting for this pub and restaurant. It is a recently named establishment and on the sign is displayed a rather sinister looking Churchill wearing Homburg hat, holding a cigar, from which smoke is wreathing, within the V formed fingers.

Churchill Public House, Chatham. There is no sign for display at this pub but inside is a very good collection of memorabilia and photographs of Churchill. It was formerly known as "Army and Navy" but with the decline of naval activity in the town it was renamed. It has a Randolph Room and a 'Winny' cocktail bar.

The Churchill Arms, Long Crendon. Some six miles from Princes Risborough and in the vicinity of Thame, Oxford is this old pub. The sign features an extremely well painted Coat of Arms of Sir Winston Churchill and there are a few photographs of him inside. The pub has borne the same name for over 130 years.

The Churchill Arms, Sturminster Marshall. This small pub is in Hampshire and has been established with its name for over 100 years.

Winstons. Situated in the heart of Bloomsbury, in Coptic Street, this restaurant and wine bar is a tribute to Churchill. it has an extremely interesting large selection of pictures, cartoons and photographs of Churchill which cover the walls. There are also some ceramic items and a collection of associated memorabilia which all combine to give a very strong Churchillian atmosphere.

The Lord Warden, Liverpool. This pub in London road is at least 150 years old and has been known by the same name since its beginning. It is puzzling that it is so named and no-one seems to know the origin of the title. It is all the more intriguing when the distance from the Cinque Ports is considered. However, the sign features a particularly fine portrait of Sir Winston hatless, wearing the Lord Warden's uniform with the Sash of the Order of the Garter.

Sir Winston Churchill Public House, Bamford. situated on the road between Bury and Rochdale, Lancashire. It is a fairly new pub, having been constructed about 1970. Considerable controversy was generated by local historians and societies when the pub was built, since the site on which it stands was formerly occupied by a very old pub which had stood there for several centuries. The old inn had had past associations with Oliver Cromwell. The signboard has a picture of Sir Winston sitting in an armchair, wearing pinstriped trousers with black jacket and gold watch chain.

Winston Churchill, Chorlton Street, Manchester. A quaint little inn which was formerly known as "The Mechanics". It was renamed "Winston Churchill" about 1978. An extremely good painting of Churchill is on the signboard which reminds one of the well-known photograph by Karsh of Ottawa.

The Sir Winston Churchill Inn, Annersley Woodhouse, Nottinghamshire. This inn was built in 1965 and as Sir Winston died that year it was named after him as a tribute. The sign featured a painting of Churchill which became very worn and was taken down for refurbishment. It has not yet been replaced.

Patriotic cloth printed 1914 presenting a gallery of allied military and political leaders very rare £50 framed.

First World War memorabilia detailed tin, £25; Bust by Lawton (sculptor) £70; wooden trinket box £45.

Satirical but prophetic German medallion, First World War. Sir Winston, 'Ruler of the Sea'. Courtesy British Museum.

Bust by Shelley, First World War. Very rare, £70/£90.

Carved caricature, skirted Churchill as Britannia. First World War. Made by disabled soldiers, rare, £100.

74

German satirical medal, the sinking of the 'Athenia,' 1939. Obverse Churchill on shipping crate.
Acknowledgements to J. Eric Engstrom/ Spink.

Reverse of the 'Athenia' medal.
Acknowledgements to J. Eric Engstrom/ Spink.

The sinking of the 'Ark Royal.' Churchill with Chamberlain and Hore-Belisha. (The aircraft carrier was sunk 1941, not 1939)
Acknowledgements to J. Eric Engstrom/ Spink.

Reverse of the German 'Ark Royal' medal.

75

The first Churchill toby made 1927 when he was Chancellor, issued with blue or green coat, rare £135.

The cheerful, confident Premier by Spode, 1941; rare, £500/£750. A few were reissued 1965 with slight colour variations (also rare).

Enamelled crown and silver charm.

Handkerchief, Churchill surrounded by allied flags, £10.

Churchill with representations of the armed forces, £10.

'Winston' handkerchief, £10.

Woven silk portrait, very rare, £25.

Bulldog jug by Bristol, £20; very fine jug made by Skerrett; rare £75/£95; china box containing set of ashtrays, £75.

Two jugs from Churchill's second term as First Lord. Jug on right is by Shorter (some marked 'Fielding'); some had musical movement, £70/£90 (more for the music). The other sphinx-like jug represents a ship's figurehead, made by Kirkland, £80/£90.

Cup, saucer and plate by Nelson Ware, 1941, £30/£40; Wedgwood Tankard, 1941, £65/£85; jug and beaker with cigar smoking Premier (common wartime transfer) £25/£30; pewter tankard issued 1980, £40. Mug on extreme left is Wedgwood item, 1965, £25/£30; beaker with etching, 1974, £15.

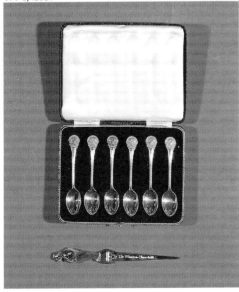

Set of silver teaspoons with Churchill's head issued 1941, £75; paper knife, 1980, £5.

Caricature of the First Lord, 1939, £40; chunky figure from set of war leaders issued 1943 by Bovey, £35. Also made in bone china.

Fine pair of matching jugs by Spode, 1941, designed by Eric Olsen, £100/£130 for Churchill, less for Roosevelt. Uncoloured versions exist.

Jug on left is by R. Winton, 'The Man of the Year,' 1941; this large size, £100/£120; other items all under £25.

Bud vase, Royal Winton, £30; Loving Cup, 1941, by Wade, £75; Beaker by Meakin, £20; Centenary Goblet, Coalport, £100; mug with Churchill handle, £25; glass tumbler, £10.

Woven portrait, very rare, approx. 36" long, £50 (the other items are shown elsewhere in this book).

 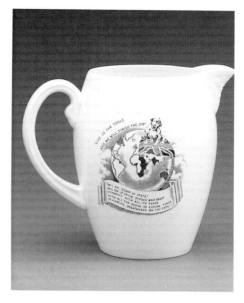

Superb jug by Spode, 1941, rare, also issued in other colours.

Reverse of Spode Jug, £150/£180, scarce item.

Ashtrays, Churchill as buoyant First Lord, 1939, rare, £100; bulldog tray, £40; tray with bust, 1970, £15; standing figure, 1954, £20; portrait dish, £5.

The beautiful Spode memorial plate, issued 1967, £100/£125. The white figure was made in India (wartime), £30; china dish with handle is by Tuscan Pottery, 1943, rare £50; tile with portrait, £10; matchbox cover, £10; First World War souvenir, £30.

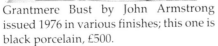

Grantmere Bust by John Armstrong issued 1976 in various finishes; this one is black porcelain, £500.

Wall plaque by Marcus, 1986, £15.

White China Bust by Oscar Nemon, made by Spode, issued 1965, £95.
Courtesy Spode Museum.

Crystal bust and black basalt bust, centenary issue, both limited editions, £300/£350 each, by Webb Corbett and Royal Doulton.

The rare Doulton two-handled jug, withdrawn soon after issue in 1940. Highly sought after piece with a price of £5000 upwards; only two colour versions known. Courtesy Royal Doulton.

Plate on left issued 1980, £10; centre item with portrait by Connie Greenwood, £100. The other plate is National Trust issue, 1984, £35.

Plate by Panorama, £20; very rare item by Vernons Kilns of U.S.A. commemorating the Atlantic Charter, 1941, £150/£200; plate by Soho Pottery, 1940, £40.

Ashtrays feature prominently among Churchill souvenirs; here is a selection in various materials, most of wartime origin, £10/£40.

The familiar Doulton jug in all three sizes, introduced 1941, still in production, £20.

Small toby jug, very rare post war, £55 (from set of Allied Leaders).

Three rare wartime figures, L-R: Lancaster China, £45; Lucitania of Portugal (similar to the Bovey figure), £45; Newport Pottery (another version of this firm's figure), £75.

Churchill dolls made by Peggy Nisbet, £25, the centre figure is a hand carved wooden caricature, £45.

Figure with stick is from India, 1942, £25; white suited item is from Doulton, £55; large bronze type figure, £50; cariacature with bulldog, 1955, £40.

Caricature figures made about 1955, many types exist, £10/£35.

Familiar wartime poster. Courtesy British Imperial War Museum.

Kitchener style poster.

Fine American poster.

Belgian cartoon.

The ace is from a Spanish pack, the other cards are wartime issue except for the signed pack which is post war, £10/£40.

Double pack issued to commemorate Churchill's retirement 1955, £40.

Playing cards issued Belgium, 1945, £15/£30.

Another Belgian pack, 1945, £15/30.

Dish with speech extract, Kent China, rare, £40; the fabulous Jarvis jug (different colour from the other in this book), £700; China box by Doulton, rare, £85/£100, wartime item.

Figure on left is by Newport Pottery, £75; the fine jug, unmarked, £85/£100; the figure on the right is from Portugal, £100; all very rare. The plaques are unmarked, £20/£30 each.

92

Gathering of jugs signifying Churchill's Naval connection.

Collection of caricature jugs.

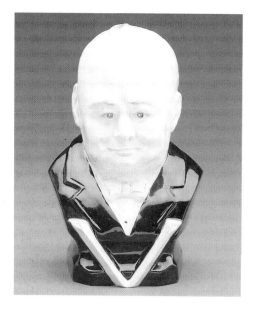

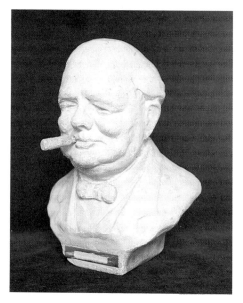

Bust by J. Edge, 1941, rare £85.

Table lighter, bust by Talent, 1941; the cigar is the striker, £40/£60. Courtesy V. Lakey.

Bust by Wedgwood, 1974, reissued in 1985 at £82.

Marble type bust by Nemon made by Alva Museum replicas, New York, £70/£90.

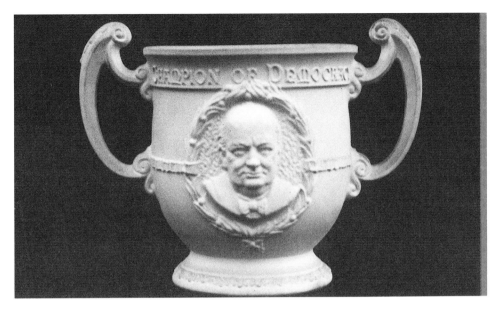

Loving cup, Burgess & Leigh, 1941; Roosevelt is on the other side, £100. Some were finished in crimson and gold, very rare, £500. Courtesy Burgess & Leigh.

Enamel on copper box by Halcyon Days, 1974, £100/£130.

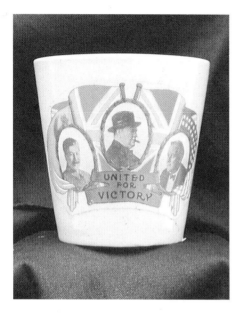

Victory beaker, very rare, £40.

Battle of Britain mug by Kent China, rare wartime item, £60/£70.

Set of tumblers, wartime leaders, £30 the set.

Metal matchbox covers popular during the war, £10.

Very rare cigar box from India, wartime item, £15/£20.

Selection of badges, these include Belgian (top left) and Danish (top right) £5/£10.

Various spoons, post war, £3/£10.

Wall mask, 1955, £15.

Wall mask, 1965, £25.

Very rare head by Minton, 1941, £200/£250.

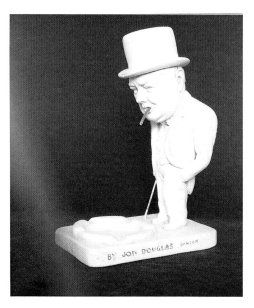

Fine caricature on ashtray by Jon Douglas, 1955, £50. Courtesy V. Lakey.

Group of items showing prominence of 'V' sign. Oval and metal plaques valued at £30/£40 each; small bust, £30; metal figure, £15; Jarvis jug, £700.

Novelty clogs from Holland, £25; miniature Burleigh jug, £45; rare cup and saucer by Paragon, £85/£100; Atlantic meeting commemorative plate, £70, rare; unmarked resin figure, £10.

Portrait busts, bookends, by Jon Douglas, 1955, £85/£100; the ashtray has a very rare transfer, made by T. G. Green, £45/£50.

White bust by Floral China, £80; plate by T. G. Green, £75/£90; plaque with Spitfire and Churchill's words, Crown Devon, £75/£90; small jug by R. Winton, £40; unmarked mask, £20.

Dish by Royal Winton, £50; plate by Burgess & Leigh, £90/£100; wall mask by Minton, £90; glass tumbler, £15. All very rare wartime pieces.

Glazed tile, spherical glass paperweight, unmarked jug, small dish, plate issued 1965 (others wartime origin) £15/£50.

Dutch liberation postcard issued 1945, £5

Excellent doll, probably formed part of mounted display, very accurate, possibly unique, £100.

Very rare continental tin, 1945, £30; Churchill as lion in bottle, very rare, possibly unique, £100.

Plate, one of a set of three which included Roosevelt and Stalin, £25. Courtesy V. Lakey.

Very rare plate, £90; tumblers also very rare, £15 each.

Churchill brand 'Bermuda' cigars, German make.

Churchill 'Brazil' cigars, German make.

Smoking related items; matchbox covers, cigars, cigar bands.

Solid brass seated figure and bust by B.E.L. Products, Birmingham, 1970, £40/£60. Courtesy B.E.L.

Victory scarf, very rare, £25.

Ashtray with angled recess which forms a 'V' when cigarettes are inserted. Extremely rare item, £50. The cartoon is by Low.

Tobacco jar by T. Lawrence, £70, rare; bust by Borthwick, £15; small figure in frame, rare, £45; treacle glazed jug, rare, £50; unmarked bust, £15.

Small bust by Lawton China, £40; character jug by Carten Scott, very rare, £100; toby jug by Lancaster Pottery, rare, £75.

Character jug, £25; portrait in relief, £30; ashtray with bust by Tunstall, £30; small Royal Winton jug, £45.

Wall mask by Goldscheider, intriguing pair of figures, Churchilland Hitler, very rare, £80; Battle of Britain calendar, £25, rare; unmarked bust, £20.

Silhouette by Baverstock, £15.

Portrait woven in Switzerland, £10.

Selection of postcards covering 40 years of Churchill's public life.

Character jug made in Portugal, £10.

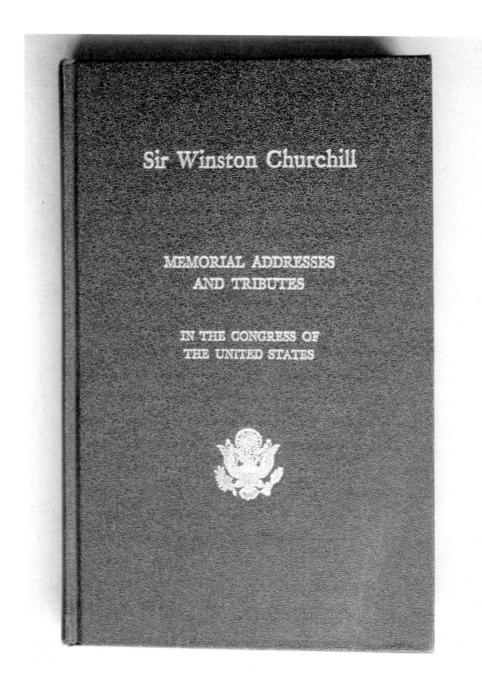

Book of American Tributes. (This book was presented to the Lord Mayor of London)

Enemy matchbox covers. Note the caricatures in skull's sockets.

Allied leaders postcard.

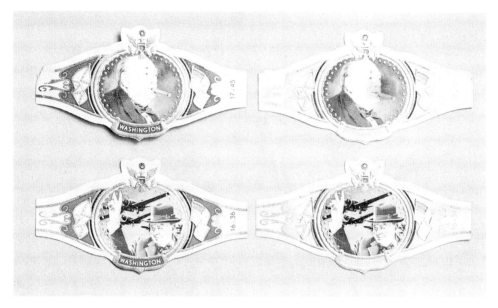

Set of cigar bands.

Wartime postal souvenirs, very rare.

Churchill on coins; from top, American dollar, Isle of Man and UK Crowns, Yemeni Riyal.

Reverses of Churchill medallions; Allied Victory medal, memorial medal, Dunkirk Anniversary medal, French Liberation medal.

Set of centenary medallions showing famous addresses of Churchill.

Medallion reverses showing diversity of designs.

Superb pair of medallions commemorating the Atlantic Conference, silver, £60.

The reverse of the Atlantic Conference medallions.

Silver medallion which opens to reveal set of circular pictures illustrating events in Churchill's life, £70, made by Toye, Kenning & Spencer.

M.P. for Oldham.   Wedding   Mobilisation of the Fleet, 1914.   In the Trenches, 1915.

Battle of Britain.   The Blitz.   Addressing the U.S. Congress.   The Funeral Cortege.

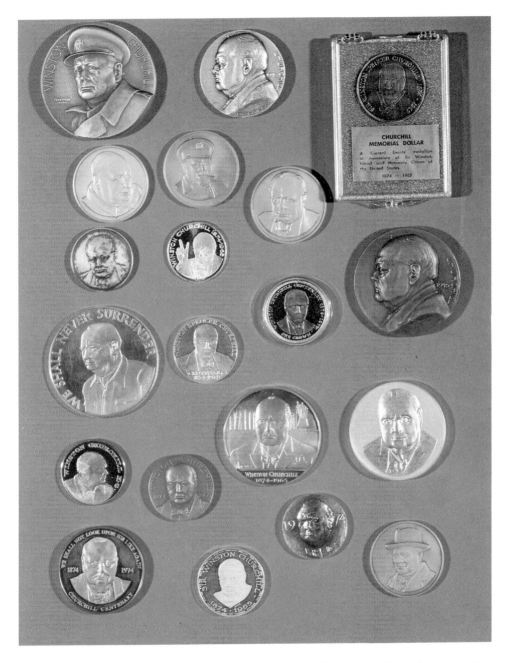

This selection shows: top left corner, French Liberation medal; the cased item is an American dollar; the piece below the dollar is the Allied Victory medal; fourth item down on extreme left is 25th Anniversary of Dunkirk; item immediately above was for Churchill's 80th birthday. The others commemorate either the death or centenary of Churchill.

The last sitting, Churchill posing for his last portrait from life, at Chartwell. The artist was Bernard Hailstone. Courtesy B. Hailstone.

Bronze plaque 24" x 18" with portrait in deep relief by Arthur Pan, 1941, £150, rare.

Stooped and brooding, symbolising the military might of Britain. Ivor Roberts-Jones magnificent statue; a familiar landmark in Parliament Square. Courtesy Ivor Roberts-Jones.

The Brunei statue outside the Churchill Museum. Astrid Zydower, Sculptress. Courtesy Brunei Museum.

The Washington statue by William McVey, being unveiled by Randolph Churchill. Photo UPI/Bettmann Newsphotos.

Franta Belsky working on the Fulton statue. This interesting picture shows some of the working models necessary to achieve the perfection which is the hallmark of Mr. Belsky's work.

The Malta Bust by Vincent Apap. Courtesy
Malta Information Dept.

The Wanstead bust by L. Froni.

The Brunei Bust by C. Sheridan. Courtesy
Brunei Museum.

The Copenhagen Bust by O. Nemon in
Winston Churchill Park.

The Belsky Bust. Courtesy Churchill Hotel, London.

The Einstein Bust. Govt. Art Collection.

Bust by Unknown sculptor. Courtesy Major Taylor-Smith.

Bust by A. Toft.

123

The Oslo Churchill still in plaster leaving the artist's studio at Cratfield for Norway in 1976. Courtesy Ivor Roberts-Jones.

The Oslo statue on site, nine feet tall it stands outside the Index Building. It was unveiled by H.M. The King of Norway. Photo. Ivor Roberts-Jones.

The New Orleans figure prior to going to the U.S.A. with the scaffold still in place. The left arm had not at the time been fixed to the figure. Courtesy Ivor Roberts-Jones.

125

As they remembered him – the eleven feet tall statue which stands in British Square, New Orleans. Courtesy Ivor Roberts-Jones.

As a boy with his beloved soldiers.

The student soldier

An old man painting

Vincent Apap discussing his work with Winston Churchill.
Photo Malta Dept. of Information.

Bronze plaque in relief, Churchill speaking from Durban's Town Hall 1899. This memorial is
in Churchill Street, Durban.
Photo Durban History Museum.

128

The brunei statue in the artist's studio prior to being shipped east. Photo Astrid Zydower.

The Fulton statue just before casting. Franta Belzky looks with pride at his majestic work. Photo Press Association.

The House of Commons statue by O. Nemon.
This defiant figure stands by the Members'
Lobby. Photo Central Office of Information.

The grim Woodford statue by David McFall.

Bust by David McFall in The Grocers' Hall, London.

Bust by Nemon in Churchill College, Cambridge University.

Bust in Bromley Library by Elsie March.

Memorial in Winston Churchill Gardens, Jersey, with bronze plaque by Anthony Gray.

The striding statue, by Nemon, at St. Margaret's Bay, Kent.

The seated Westerham statue, by Nemon, just two miles from Chartwell.

Another double statue by Nemon in Blenheim Palace.

The Luxembourg statue situated in Winston Churchill Place, by Nemon. Courtesy Phototheque de la Ville de Luxembourg.

Fine sculpture by Karin Churchill (no relation). (Edition of 400 not yet completed)

134

The Halifax, Nova Scotia statue by Nemon. Courtesy Public Archives, Nova Scotia.

Another view of the Halifax statue. Courtesy Public Archives, Nova Scotia.

Churchill in the uniform of Elder Brother of
Trinity House by Oswald Birley. Courtesy
Trinity House.

Wearing the uniform of Lord Warden of the
Cinque Ports, copied in 1960 by John Leigh-
Pemberton from Oswald Birley's portrait.

Portrait by Alfred Eggerton Cooper.
Courtesy Courtaulds Institute.

Portrait by Arthur Hayward about 1946; in Kent University.

The controversial portrait by Sutherland which was destroyed on Lady Churchill's instructions. Courtesy National Portrait Gallery.

Portrait by Max Nauta which hangs in the Dutch Houses of Parliament. Courtesy

Painted about 1915 by James Guthrie. Courtesy National Galleries of Scotland.

Siren suited Churchill by Frank Salisbury. Courtesy National Trust.

Portrait by Bernard Hailstone R.P. American owned. Courtesy B. Hailstone.

The young Churchill by Edwin Ward, about 1901.

Portrait by Oswald Birley about 1951. Courtesy National Trust.

Impression by Walter Sickert 1927. Courtesy National Portrait Gallery.

Study by G. Sutherland 1954. Courtesy National Portrait Gallery.

Epic painting by Sir James Guthrie completed 1930 after six years work and research. Entitled 'Some British Statesmen of the First World War'. Courtesy National Portrait Gallery.

Excellent portrait by Douglas Chandor 1946. Painted at the request of President Truman. Churchill wears Royal Air Force uniform with the rank of honorary Air Commodore. Courtesy National Portrait Gallery, Smithsonian Institute, Washington.

142

Very fine drawing of the First Lord of the Admiralty and the First Sea Lord. By S. Begg,
December 1914. Courtesy Illustrated London News.

Churchill as Secretary of State for War and Air, November 1919.
Drawn by Steven Spurrier. Courtesy Illustrated London News.

Painting by John Leigh-Pemberton after a wartime photograph. Courtesy Whitbread's Brewery.

Churchill relaxing, painting, from a photograph by John Leigh-Pemberton. Courtesy Whitbread's Brewery.

144

The 'Big Three' in conference at Yalta, 1943 painted by an unknown Russian artist. Courtesy National Trust.

On board H.M.S. 'Prince of Wales' August, 1941, painted by Raymond Wilson from a photograph. Courtesy Trinity House.

Copied by John Leigh-Pemberton from William Orpen's 1915 portrait. Courtesy Churchill College, Cambridge.

Impression by Sutherland from the 1954 sittings. Courtesy Beaverbrook Art Gallery, New Brunswick.

146

AFTER A PHOTO-ETCHING (BY SPECIAL PROCESS) BY JAMES BACON AND SONS, OF NEW BOND STREET AND NEWCASTLE-ON-TYNE.

THE MINISTER TO WHOM THE TAXPAYER LOOKS FOR RELIEF UNDER THE FORTHCOMING BUDGET: THE RIGHT HON. WINSTON CHURCHILL. P.C., M.P., C.H., CHANCELLOR OF THE EXCHEQUER.

Etching of Churchill used on the front cover of the 'Illustrated London News', April 1925. Very fine portrait produced by James Bacon & Sons. Courtesy Illustrated London News.

Churchill as Chancellor of the Duchy of Lancaster soon after his resignation from the admiralty. Courtesy Illustrated London News.

Mosaic Churchill on the floor of the National Gallery, superb work by Boris Anrep. Reproduced by Courtesy of the Trustees of the National Gallery, London. Copyright, The Victoria and Albert Museum.

AFTER HIS "ORAN" SPEECH: MR. CHURCHILL CHEERED BY THE HOUSE.

SPECIALLY DRAWN FOR "THE ILLUSTRATED LONDON NEWS" BY TERENCE CUNEO.

Terence Cuneo's depiction of the scene in Parliament after Churchill's inspiring 'Oran' speech,
July 1940. Courtesy Illustrated London News.

149

The figure on view about 1980.

The first wax figure of Churchill made 1908. Courtesy Madame Tussauds.

The Churchill wax figure on display at Louis Tussaud, Copenhagen. Courtesy Louis Tussaud.

Figure made about 1965, this wax portrait was lent to various exhibitions overseas. Modelled by Bernard Tussaud. Courtesy Madame Tussauds.

The current wax portrait on display at Madame Tussauds.

The wax Churchill in Madame Tussauds, Amsterdam. Courtesy Madame Tussauds, Amsterdam.

The wax Churchill which was on display in the early 1960's. The robes are now on loan to Chartwell. Courtesy Madame Tussauds.

Churchill at Churchill, Somerset.

Sir Winston Churchill, Dunstable.   Former sign.

Winston Churchill, Ide Hill, Kent.

The Churchill, Paxford, Chipping Camden.

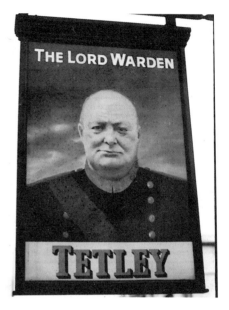

The Churchill, West Lavington, Nr. Devizes.
Courtesy Bass.

The Lord Warden, London Road, Liverpool.
Courtesy Stephen Hart.

Churchills, Silvertown, London.

'The Winston Churchill'. New sign at Dunstable.

The Churchill Arms, Kensington Church Street, London.

The Churchill, Chorlton Street, Manchester.

Sir Winston Churchill, Hutton, Nr Shenfield, Essex.

The Winston Churchill, Debden. One side of the board.

The Winston Churchill, Debden. The other side of the board.

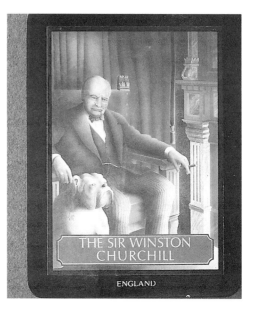

The Sir Winston Churchill, Bamford, Lancashire. Sign showing signs of wear.

The Sir Winston Churchill, locality unknown.

APPENDIX

The Rt. Hon. Sir Winston Leonard Spencer Churchill,
K.G. 1953; P.C. 1907; O.M. 1946; C.H. 1922; F.R.S. 1941;
Born 30 November 1874, elder son of Rt. Hon. Lord Randolph Churchill, 3rd
son of the 7th Duke of Marlborough.
Married 1908, Clementine, G.B.E., daughter of late Col. Sir H.M. Hozier,
K.C.B., 3rd Dragoon Guards.
Children, 1 son, 4 daughters.
Educated: Harrow, Sandhurst.

Military History

Entered Army, 1895; served with Spanish Forces in Cuba 1895 1st Class
(Spanish) Order of Military Merit); served, attached 31st Punjab Infantry, with
Malakand Field Force, 1897, (Despatches, medal with clasp); served as
orderly officer to Sir W. Lockhart with Tirah Expeditionary force, 1898 (Clasp);
served, attached 21st Lancers, with Nile Expeditionary force, 1898, present at
Battle of Khartoum (medal with clasp); served as Lieut. South African Lt.
Horse; acted as correspondent Morning Post, South Africa, 1899-1900; taken
prisoner, action 15 November, but escaped 12 December; present at actions of
Acton Homes, Venter's Spruit, Hussar Hill, Cingolo, Monte Cristo, and at
Battles of Spion Kop, Vaal Krantz and Pieters; engagements of Johannesburg
and Diamond Hill, and capture of Pretoria (medal with six clasps); Late Lieut,
the 4th Queen's Own Hussars; Major, Queen's Own Oxfordshire Hussars;
Lieut. Col. commanding 6th Royal Scots Fusiliers, France, 1916 (medals);
retired 1916.

Political History

Contested (C) Oldham, 1899; M.P. (C) Oldham 1900-04, (L) 1904-06; (L) N.W.
Manchester, 1906-08; (L) Dundee 1908-1918. (Co-L) 1918-22; (Const.) Epping
Div. of Essex, 1924-31; (C) 1931-45; (C) Woodford 1945-64.

Under Secretary of State for the Colonies, 1906-08; President Board of Trade,
1908-10; Home Secretary, 1910-11; First Lord of the Admiralty, 1911-15;
Chancellor of the Duchy of Lancaster, 1915; Minister of Munitions, 1917;
Secretary of State for War and Air, Jan. 1919-Feb. 1921; Air and the Colonies,
Feb-Apl 1921; and for the Colonies until Oct. 1922; Chancellor of the

Exchequer, 1924-1929; First Lord of the Admiralty, 1939-1940; Prime Minister, First Lord of the Treasury and Minister of Defence, 1940-1945; Leader of the Opposition, 1945-51; Prime Minister and First Lord of the Treasury, Oct. 1951-1955. Resigned Apl. 1955; was also Minister of Defence Oct. 1951-Jan. 1952.

Honorary Appointments

Elder Brother of Trinity House, 1913-; Lord Warden of the Cinque Ports, 1941-; Lord Rector of Aberdeen University, 1914-1918, of Edinburgh University, 1929-1932; Chancellor of Bristol University, 1929; Hon. Fellow Merton College, Oxford, 1942; Chairman of the Trustees, Churchill College, Cambridge, 1959; First Hon. Fellow of Churchill College, Cambridge, 1964; Hon Bencher Gray's Inn, 1942; Grand Master Primrose League, 1943-; Hon. Academician Extraordinary of R.A., 1948; One-man show at Royal Academy, 1959; Hon. R.B.A.; F.R.I.B.A., 1941; Hon. F.R.C.S. 1943; F.Z.S. 1944; F.R.Ae.S. ,1944; F.S.E., 1946; F.R.S.L., 1947; F.R.G.S., 1948; F.J.I., 1950; Hon. F.R.C.P., 1951; Hon. F.B.A.,1952; Hon. A.R.C.V.S., 1955; Hon.F.I.O.B., 1962; Hon Member: of Lloyds; of Instn. of Municipal and County Engrs; of R. Inst. of Naval Architects; of Instn. of Mining and Metallurgy; Hon. Pres. U.N.Assoc.: Pres. Constitutional Club; Vice-Pres. R.A.F. Benevolent Fund, 1919-; Vice-Pres. London Library, 1948-; First President of the Victoria Cross Association, 1959. Liverymen of Mercers' Co.; Hon. Freeman of Shipwrights' Co.; Hon. Life Member of Assoc. of Men of Kent and Kentish Men; D.L. Kent, 1949; Pres. Franco-British Soc., 1951; Patron, Bucks Club, 1952; a Vice-Pres. Soc. of the Friends of St. George's and Descendants of the Knights of the Garter, 1953; Hon. Pres. Amateur Fencing Assoc. 1953; Pres. Westerham Br. British Legion, 1953; Col. 4th Queen's Own Hussars, 1941-58; Col. The Queen's Royal Irish Hussars, 1958-; Hon. Air Cdre. No. 615 (Co. of Surrey) Fighter Squadron., R.Aux. A.F., 1939-.; Hon. Col. 63rd Oxf. Yeo. Anti-Tank Regt. R.A. (T.A.), 1942; 6th Bn. R. Scots Fus., 1940; 479 (Cinque Ports) H.A.A. Regt., R.A. (T.A.) 1947; 299 Fd. Regt. R.A. (Bucks and Oxf. Yeo.),T.A.; 4th/5th (Cinque Ports) Bn. R. Sussex Regt., 1941: 1st/4th Bn. Essex Regt., 1945; 6th (Cinque Ports) Cadet Bn. Buffs; Member of the Jockey Club, 1950; Grand Seigneur of the Hudson's Bay Company, 1956; Hon. Life Member Friendship Veterans Fire Engine Company of Alexandria, Virginia, U.S.A.,1960.

Medals

India 1895, Sudan 1896/7, South Africa, Queen Victoria's Medal 1899/1902, 1914-15 Star, British War Medal 1914-20, Victory Medal, 1939-45 Star, Africa Star, Italy Star, France and Germany Star, Defence Medal.

Awards

Special Award, Sept. 1945, Albert Gold Medal of R. Soc. of Arts, 1945; Grotius Medal (Netherlands) 1949; Sunday Times Literary Award and Medal, 1938 and 1949; Nobel Prize for Literature, 1953; Charlemange Prize, 1955; Freedom House Award (U.S.A.), 1955; Williamsburg Award, 1955; Franklin Medal of City of Philadelphia, 1956; Humanitarian Award for 1954, 1956; Theodor Herzl Award, Zionist Organisation of America, 1964.

Honorary Degrees

D.C.L.: Oxford, 1925, Rochester, U.S.A., 1941. Doctor of Laws: Queen's Belfast, 1926, Bristol, 1929, Harvard, 1943, Mcgill, Canada, 1944, Brussels, Louvain, 1945, Miami, U.S.A., Westminster College U.S.A., Columbia, U.S.A., Aberdeen, Leyden, 1946, St. Andrews, 1948. liverpool, 1949, University of New York State, 1954; D.Phil. and Hist., Oslo, 1948; Litt. D., Cambridge, 1948; D. Litt., London, 1948; D.Phil., Copenhagen, 1950.

Freedoms

Oldham, 1941; Edinburgh, 1942; City of London, 1943; Wanstead and Woodford, Brussels, Antwerp, 1945; Aberdeen, City of Westminster, Luxembourg, Blackpool, Birmingham, Beckenham, Stafford, 1946; Darlington, Ayr, Woodstock, Brighton, Manchester, 1947; Eastbourne, Perth, Aldershot, Cardiff, 1948; Kensington, Strasbourg, 1949; Bath, Worcester, Wimbledon, Portsmouth, 1950; Sheffield, Aberystwyth, Malden and Coombe, Deal, Dover, 1951; Leeds, 1953; Poole, 1954; Rochester, Londonderry, Belfast, Harrow, 1955; Douglas (I.O.M.), Margate, Hastings, 1957; Estcourt (Natal), 1964;

Honorary Citizen

Cuba, 1941; Pinar Del Rio (Cuba), 1942; Paris, 1945; Athens, Marathon, Thebes, Aeglion, 1945; Naupactos (Gr.), 1946; Jacksonville, Florida, 1949; Nancy, 1950; Roquebrune-Cap Martin (A.-M), 1956; U.S.A. and individual States of Maryland, Hawaii, West Virginia, New Hampshire, Nebraska, Tennessee, N. Carolina, 1963; Hon. Mayor Cap d'Ail (A.-M), 1952; Gold Medals of Cities of New York, Amsterdam and Rotterdam, 1946. Member, National Congress of American Indians, 1963.

Foreign Decorations

Knight Grand Cross, Order of Leopold of Belgium; Ordre Knight Grand Cross, Order of the Netherlands Lion; Grand Cross Orde Grand-Ducal de la Couronne de Chene of Luxembourg; Grand Cross with Chain, Order of St. Olav, Norway; Kt., Order of Elephant, Denmark; Danish Liberation Medal; French Croix de Guerre avec Palme (1914); Belgian Croix de Guerre avec Palme (1915); Medaille Militaire of France; Mil. Medal of Luxembourg; Spanish Order of Mil. Merit (1st. cl.); Spanish Medal Cuban Campaign 1895-98; Khadives Sudan Medal 1896; D.S.M.(U.S.A.); U.S.A.F. Pilot's Wings; Fr. Croix de la Liberation; Order of Star of Nepal; Grand Sash of the High Order of Sayyid Mohammed bin Ali al Senussi.

Publications

The Story of the Malakand Field Force, 1898; The River War, 1899; Savrola, 1900; London to Ladysmith via Pretoria, 1900; Ian Hamilton's March, 1900; Lord Randolph Churchill, 1906; My African Journey, 1908; Liberalism and the Social Problem; The World Crisis, 4 vols. 1923-1929; My Early Life, 1930; The Eastern Front, 1931; Thoughts and Adventures, 1932; Marlborough, vol. 1,1933; vol. 2,1934;vol. 3,1936; vol. 4,1938; Great Contemporaries, 1937; Arms and the Covenant (Speeches), 1938; Step by Step, 1939; Into Battle (Speeches), 1941; The Unrelenting Struggle (Speeches), 1942; The End of the Beginning (Speeches), 1943; Onwards to Victory (Speeches), 1944; The Dawn of Liberation (speeches), 1945; Victory, 1946; Secret Session (Speeches), 1946; The Sinews of Peace (Speeches), 1948; Painting as a Pastime, 1948; Europe Unite (Speeches), 1950; In the Balance (Speeches), 1951; Stemming the Tide (Speeches 1951-1952), 1953; The Unwritten Alliance (Speeches), 1954, 1961; The Second World War, vol. 1, The Gathering Storm, 1948; vol. 2, Their Finest Hour, 1949, vol. 3, The Grand Alliance, 1950; vol. 4, The Hinge of Fate, 1951; vol. 5, Closing the ring, 1952; vol. 6, Triumph and Tragedy, 1954; A History of the English Speaking Peoples; vol. 1, The Birth of Britain, 1956; vol. 2, the New World, 1956; vol. 3, the Age of Revolution, 1957; vol. 4, The Great Democracies, 1958; Frontiers and Wars, 1962 (Repr. in one vol.) Malakand Field Force, The River War, London to Ladysmith and Ian Hamilton's March, slightly abridged).

160

The most recent toby jug of Winston Churchill, modelled by Peggy Davies and commissioned by Kevin Francis Ceramics Ltd, a limited edition to be issued in 1989.

Dashing portrait painted 1915 by Ernest Townsend; it hangs in the National Liberal Club.

Painting by Lavery which hangs at Chartwell. Churchill with the French steel helmet which he favoured in 1915. Courtesty National Trust.

Cartoon which appeared in Vanity Fair about 1900 by Spy.

Exceptionally fine, detailed figure of Churchill outside No. 10 Downing Street, June 4th, 1940. Modelled by A. Turner, made by Ashmor, Worcester. Commissioned by the History in Porcelain Co. authenticated by Lady Soames and the International Churchill Society. £600

Close up view showing superb detail of the History in Porcelain figure.

The Foley 'Intarsio' teapot with the lid on. Value £800/£1000.

166

Plate made about 1914, backstamp CETEM ware, the cartoon is by Miguet - one of a series. Exceedingly rare plate, £250 plus.

Wall mask, unmarked; the splendid Burgess & Leigh plate, which is very rare (the other one in this book is red), £100; bust by Tom Bayley, £25.

Churchill wearing the Robes of Chancellor of Bristol University. This painting, by Frank Salisbury, hangs in the University. Courtesy Bristol University.

MAY GOD DEFEND THE RIGHT

Very attractive toby jug made 1941 by Wilkinsons, the modeller was Clarice Cliff. About 200 or so were made, the price today is round about £1000.

Painting by Bernard Hailstone of Churchill in the uniform of Lord Warden of the Cinque Ports. Courtesy Bernard Hailstone.

Second World War postcards, all except for the top left corner card are continental issue about the time of the Liberation, but the centre card bottom row is an anti-Churchill Flemish card. Most of these are quite rare.

A selection of cigarette cards spanning some 40 years reflecting the continuous prominence of Churchill.

The splendid Bulldog by Crown Devon Pottery, very rare, £130/£160.

The Doulton Bulldog, c.1943 (with cigar and hat) was available in two sizes, the smaller shown here is valued at £200.

The only known ceramic item showing Churchill as the Bulldog. Unmarked and extremely rare, £90/£120.

Relaxing during a visit to 3rd Div. at Schloss Moyland after the crossing of the Rhine. Painted by George A. Campbell. Courtesy 'After the Battle' Magazine.

This portrait is by Professor Arthur Pan, 1942. It was reproduced to be sold to raise funds for Mrs. Churchill's 'Aid to Russia Fund'. Courtesy Frost & Reed Ltd.

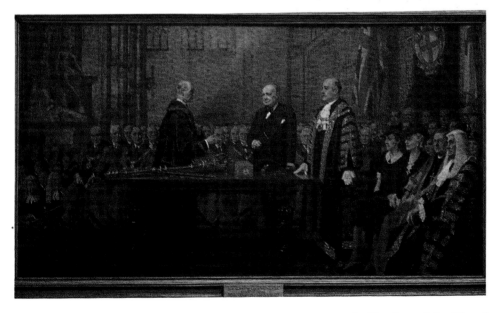

A major work by Frank Salisbury showing Churchill receiving the Freedom of the City of London, June, 1943. Courtesy Guildhall Library.

Portrait of Churchill by Salisbury which hangs in the headquarters of the Jockey Club, Newmarket. Courtesy The Jockey Club.

176

SIR WINSTON L. SPENCER CHURCHILL KG OM CH MP
HONORARY FREEMAN OF DEAL 1951-1965

This portrait by Dennis Ramsay Esq.
was acquired by public subscription
and presented to Deal Borough Council
on 24th October 1987

Another study of the Lord Warden's colourful uniform worn by Churchill, this time by Dennis Ramsay. This portrait hangs in Deal Town Hall. Courtesy Deal Town Council.

The superb Leonard Jarvis jug made about 1947, rare, £700.

This is known as the last portrait from life. It was painted in 1955 by Bernard Hailstone. Courtesy B. Hailstone.

The graceful Abbeyvale Chalice, 1965, worth in the region of £1000. Courtesy Britannia Antiques.

One of the rarest toby jugs of Churchill, unmarked but believed to be made by Floral China.

Splendid lidded urn made 1965 by Coalport, the number issued was 125, which makes it fairly rare and the price of issue was £125; the value today is around £1000.

Sombre seated statue by Oscar Nemon in the Guildhall, London. The first major statue of Churchill.

Quartet by E. T. Bailey for Burgess & Leigh, the jugs are wartime issue. The white figure was made when Churchill died, poignantly entitled, 'The Last Battle'.

Set of cigar bands showing Churchill's extensive range of headwear. £20 framed.

Very colourful sheet of stamps issued for the centenary of Churchill's birth in 1974.

This fine study of Winston Churchill is by Bruno Merli. It was made in 1974 in Florence; Capo di Monte. It has a value today of £600.

Bronze replicas: extreme left is the Fulton statue, £80; centre item is the Parliament Square figure, £95; large figure is by John Letts, £100; the china figure on left was made in Portugal, 1941, very rare, £300/£350; other figure is by Beswick, also very rare, £100/£125.

Gathering of tobies: left item is by Brannam, 1941, £100; top hatted figure next to it is by Kirkland, 1943, £150 and the small naval jug in front is from Thorley, £50.

187

Decanter, tray and goblets, silver, issued by Mappin and Webb for the centenary. Courtesy Mappin and Webb Ltd.

Most attractive jug made 1943 by Beswick, the designer was Frank Potts. This jug was in fact issued without a hat, having a lid which formed the top of the head; rare, £150/£175.

Churchill in R.A.F. uniform, very latinised portrayal by Sureda of Spain; interesting, if inaccurate, item, £50.

190

Sensitive portrayal of Churchill when Leader of the Opposition in 1946. The artist is Oswald Birley. Courtesy Dept. of the Environment.

Superb figure by Michael Sutty, Churchill in the uniform of the 4th Hussars. Absolutely accurate in every detail. Issued 1988 at £500

A Selection of the Hundreds of Colourful and Artistic Postage Stamps issued by many countries mainly between 1965 → 1974

195

THE WARTIME JOURNEYS ABROAD OF MR. CHURCHILL

November, 1939 Paris
January, 1940 Paris
February, 1940 Paris
16 May, 1940 Paris
22 May, 1940 Paris
31 May, 1940 Paris
June, 1940 Orleans
August, 1941 Placentia Bay, Newfoundland, Iceland.
December, 1941 Washington, Ottawa
June, 1942 Washington
August, 1942 Gibraltar, Cairo, visit to El Alamein positions, Teheran, Moscow, Cairo, Gibraltar
January, 1943 Casablanca, Marrakesh, Cairo, Turkish Syrian border, Cyprus, Cairo, Libya,Algiers
May, 1943 Washington, Gibraltar, Algiers
August, 1943 Quebec, Washington
October, 1943 Malta, Alexandria, Cairo, Teheran, Cairo, Tunis, Marrakesh
June, 1944 Normandy
July, 1944 France, visit to parts of British Front and Air Stations
August, 1944 France, visit to Battlegrounds
August, 1944 Naples, Corsica then by H.M.S. "Kimberley" to observe landings in the South of France, Italy, visit to the Fronts, Rome.
September, 1944 Quebec
October, 1944 Naples, Moscow
November, 1944 Paris
December, 1944 Athens
January, 1945 Malta, Yalta, Athens, Cairo
March, 1945 Visit to General Montgomery's H.Q. and cross the Rhine
July, 1945 Bordeaux, Berlin, Potsdam

Bibliography

Brears, C.D. Horsebrasses, Country Life Book of Antiques, Hamlyn Publishing Group Ltd. Feltham, 1981

Broad, Lewis. Winston Churchill, Hutchinson, London, 1941.

Churchill, Winston S. The Second World War vols. 1 — 6 Cassell & Co. Ltd., London, 1948-1954.

Churchill, Winston S. World Crisis, 4 vols. 1923 — 1929, Thornton, Butterworth

Churchill, Winston, S. My Early Life, Thornton Butterworth 1930

Colville, John and others, Action This Day, Working with Churchill, Macmillan, London, 1968

Engstrom, J. Eric. Medallic Portraits of Sir Winston Churchill, Spink & Son, Ltd. 1972.

Feddon, Robin. Churchill and Chartwell, National Trust, 1982.

Gilbert, Martin. Churchill, A Biography, Park Lane Press, London, 1979

MacGowan, Norman. My Years with Churchill, Souvenir Press, London, 1958

Moran, Lord. Churchill. A Struggle for Survival,
Constable & Co. Ltd., London, 1966

Morton, H.V. Atlantic Meeting, Methuen, London, 1943.

Nel, Elizabeth. Mr. Churchill's Secretary, Hodder & Stoughton, London, 1958

New York Times, Churchill in Memoriam, Bantam Inc., New York, 1965

Pugh, H.D.G. Naval Ceramics, Ceramic Book Co. Newport, Mon, 1971

Thomson, W.A. I was Churchill's Shadow, Christopher Johnson, London, 1953

Thomson, W.A. Sixty Minutes with Churchill, Christopher Johnson, London, 1951

Thomson, Malcolm, The Life and Times of Winston Churchill, Odhams Press, London, 1945.

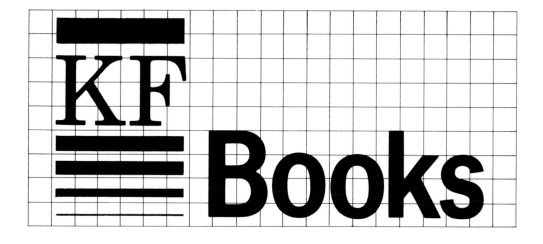

Kevin Francis Publishing
85 Landcroft Road
East Dulwich
London SE22 9JS
Telephone: 01-693 1841

CHARLOTTE RHEAD
Potter and Designer
Bernard Bumpus

The first comprehensive book on one of the major pottery designers of the 1930s. She ranks among Suzie Cooper and Clarice Cliff as a pottery artist and innovator in her own right, and indeed came from a famous family of potters.

Now at last is a major insight into Charlotte Rhead's work as she moved from pottery to pottery, taking her talents with her to produce a striking variety of work (particularly in tube-lining), which is so distinctively hers.

This book, with it's manifold illustrations and its carefully researched insight into Rhead's activities, provides the essential reference to a more complete picture of Staffordshire pottery of the 1930s.

Hardback, 150 pages, 215mm x 155mm, 30 colour plates
Price: £9.95   OUT NOW   ISBN 0 9510768 9 2

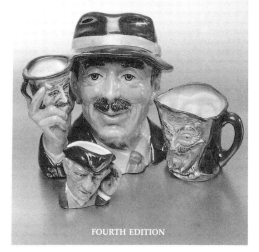

**THE CHARACTER JUG
COLLECTORS HANDBOOK**
4th Edition
128 pages, 32 colour
ISBN 1870703-05-7
by Kevin Pearson
212mm x 148mm

£9.95 softback

**THE DOULTON FIGURE
COLLECTORS HANDBOOK**
2nd Edition
144 pages, 32 colour
ISBN 0-9510768-76
by Kevin Pearson
212mm x 148mm

£8.95 softback

COLLECTING CLARICE CLIFF
1st Edition
128 pages with 90 colour plates
ISBN 1-870703-10-3
by Howard Watson
240mm x 170mm

£12.95 softback

205

So Much Is Owed

The Winston Churchill Toby, as depicted by Peggy Davies, the leading Staffordshire modeller. The grim determination of Churchill during the war years is wonderfully captured, with Churchill wearing the familiar black hat and jacket, and striped trousers. At his left side is the British Lion, symbolising the spirit of Britain and in keeping with the Latin inscription around the base: "So Much is Owed" and the quotation "The Nation had the Lion's Heart, I Provided the Roar."
On Churchill's right is the book "The History of the English Speaking Peoples"; a history of which he himself became such a large part. This book contributed to the Nobel Prize for Literature awarded him in 1953. On the back of the Toby is an intricately modelled Union Jack which forms the handle and sweeps around the back of Churchill onto the book.
In all, this Toby represents one of the finest ever made of Winston Churchill, and it is fittingly produced fifty years after he was recalled to the war effort at the Admiralty –in 1939.

The Winston Churchill Toby (Black)

The Winston Churchill Toby (White)

The White Winston Toby reflects the colourful character that Churchill was; always ready to dress in the clothing that suited the occasion, be it a uniform, a sailors outfit, a suit, or the robes of his Knighthood. Churchill was a flambouyant and exhilarating character and this Toby reflects that 'other' side of his nature.

Each Toby has been painstakingly hand painted by the most skilled of Staffordshire painters and paintresses. From beginning to end only the highest standards are used to make this one of the finest collectors Toby jugs made this century.

These Tobies are available in a limited edition of 5,000 worldwide.
The price is *£99.95 inclusive of VAT and Post & Packing, or £180.00 for the pair.
To place your order or for further details write to:

Head Office:

LONDON

Kevin Francis Ceramics Ltd/
85 Landcroft Road
London SE22 9JS
Tel: 01-693 9184

USA

Kevin Francis
13540 North Florida Avenue
Suite 103, Tampa
Florida 33613
Toll Free: 1800 634 0431

CANADA

Kevin Francis
10 Centre Street
Markham
Ontario L3P 2NH
Tel: 416 4711 999

*This price subject to change from January 1990

WE SHALL NEVER FORGET
1939 – 1945

COMMEMORATIVE PLATE

Kevin Francis plan to produce this striking commemorative plate. The limited edition size is 2500, the price is only £19.95 including VAT and Postage & Packing.

For further details write to:
Kevin Francis Ceramics
85 Landcroft Road
East Dulwich
London SE22 9JS.